Controversies in

Real Property Valuation:

A Commentary

Harold D. Albritton, MAI

American Institute of Real Estate Appraisers

430 N. Michigan Ave., Chicago, Illinois 60611

FOR EDUCATIONAL PURPOSES ONLY

The opinions and statements set forth herein are those of the author and do not necessarily reflect the viewpoint of the American Institute of Real Estate Appraisers or its individual members, and neither the Institute nor its editors and staff assume responsibility for such expressions of opinion or statements.

ISBN: 0-911780-60-2

Printed in U.S.A.

Foreword

The American Institute of Real Estate Appraisers is pleased to publish this collection of essays by Harold D. Albritton, in which he explores why various individuals appraising the same parcel of real property may arrive at different value conclusions. He brings to this volume insight on the issue of value divergencies and the benefit of his practical experience in the field of real estate appraising. Some of the essays are original in this work, while others have been published elsewhere. All have been revised and reorganized to focus more sharply on the author's goal "that appraisers will be aware of existing controversy and strive to improve the quality of appraisal services rendered."

John D. Dorchester, Jr., MAI
1982 President
American Institute of Real Estate Appraisers

About the Author

Harold D. Albritton is president of Albritton, Schultz & Associates, a real estate consulting firm in Atlanta, Georgia, specializing in income property appraisal. He is also a principal in The Real Estate Counseling Group of America.

Mr. Albritton has been a member of the Appraisal Institute since 1970 and has served on various local, regional, and national Institute committees and been a member of the Institute's faculty. He has been a member of the Editorial Board of *The Appraisal Journal* since 1975 and served on the Institute's Governing Council from 1978 to 1980. He also holds the SREA designation of the Society of Real Estate Appraisers.

Contents

Introduction

Many facets of the real estate appraisal process require judgment, after certain basic data have been gathered and analyzed. Appraisers differ substantially in appraisal knowledge and general education and have varying amounts and types of appraisal experience. Accordingly, the appraisal discipline is not a scientific method whereby one may predict with complete confidence that two or more appraisers will produce identical or reasonably approximate value estimates.

Attorneys, accountants, lenders, developers, investors, courts, and others who use the services of appraisers often become concerned when appraisers differ in their interpretation of basic valuation concepts and principles and their use of appraisal procedures.

This book has been written for both the appraiser and the nonappraiser. The nonappraiser is perhaps of major concern in this volume, but, the experienced appraiser will also find ideas, concepts, and procedures which may be useful in future appraisal or consultation assignments. Little has been written to suggest to users of appraisal services that appraisers can legitimately express divergent opinions of value or use varying methods and techniques in analyzing the same property or similar property types.

This book is designed to provide insights into numerous topics, some of which are either so controversial or so unique that the typical appraiser might have extreme difficulty in supporting a value conclusion.

Much controversy among appraisers and between appraisers and their clients relates to value definitions, concepts of economic use, and certain economic/valuation principles. Because controversy exists, it is logical to anticipate that value divergencies will occur. These topics are specifically addressed in Section 1.

1

Section 2 investigates certain areas of the appraisal process, including the traditional value approaches and usage which has been observed to reflect various degrees of divergency or controversy.

Section 3 reflects special valuation and analysis problems with which appraisers and certain nonappraisers may frequently be confronted. This section is not exhaustive as there are many other topics that legitimately might be added.

Because the book is directed to both appraisers and nonappraisers, some portions may be rather basic for the experienced appraiser, and others somewhat technical for the nonappraiser. In such instances, an effort has been made to moderate the degree of technicality.

This book addresses several issues which are of paramount significance to typical appraisal clients and to appraisers who wish to become more knowledgeable about areas of possible controversy. A knowledge of these differences may help those utilizing appraisal services to discuss appraisal assignments, improve the review of various types of appraisal reports, and promote better examination of appraisal experts in courts of law. It is also hoped that professional appraisers will be aware of existing controversy and strive to improve the quality of appraisal services rendered.

ROLES OF THE APPRAISER AND CONSULTANT

A real property appraiser is perceived as one who develops a substantiated opinion regarding one or more types of value; a counselor is one who provides guidance or recommendations for selecting one among several possible courses of action involving real estate matters.

As real estate is a major function of many businesses and industries, there is a necessity for several classifications of real property appraisers, particularly in staff, review, and independent capacities.

Staff appraisers employed by banks, insurance companies, and industry are usually responsible to individuals or committees charged with 1) underwriting mortgages; 2) acquisition, development, or disposition of operational facilities; or 3) management of real estate investment portfolios. Tax assessors of city, county, and state agencies often employ staff appraisers to assist in establishing tax bases and equalizing taxes. Local, state, and federal agencies, charged with responsibilities for acquiring privately owned property rights for public use, often employ staff appraisal personnel to estimate just compensation or to review reports provided by independent appraisers.

Staff appraisers are customarily employed to provide opinions and guidance which enable their employers to make decisions consistent with the organization's objectives. Some staff appraisers have unrestricted freedom of judgment, while others are expected to be biased. Many staff appraisers want to provide unbiased opinions but may be subjected to discriminatory employment threats.

Review appraisers are usually employed by agencies or corporations to certify that the work product of staff and independent appraisers complies with established criteria for content and procedures.

Independent, or "fee," appraisers provide appraisal services to a diverse clientele for a fee. The professional fee appraiser is independent and will not allow any personal bias or external pressure from clients, other individuals, or circumstances to influence the value conclusion. Industry and commerce have developed great confidence that the true professional will decline an assignment unless the valuation judgment is totally free from external pressures and circumstances.

The role of the independent appraiser is usually to provide a value estimate, which will assist the client in making a decision, based on a definition of the problem and an analysis of the economics of the area and the property. Many appraisal assignments require the estimation of market value of fee simple ownership interests. Frequently, partial and undivided ownership interests or valuation subject to leases, easements, existing indebtedness, or other encumbrances are involved.

The professional appraiser also may be retained to estimate other types of value or to prepare market studies, optimum use analyses, and impact studies reflecting the probable benefits or damages resulting from a specific development.

Much of the fee appraiser's time and effort is expended in data search and analysis. The validity of an appraisal is directly related to the quality of data and the appraiser's qualifications and experience, all of which are necessary to analyze the data properly in relation to the specific appraisal subject.

A real estate counselor is usually an independent person with broad experience in valuation and various other real estate disciplines such as management, development, marketing, and finance. The professional consultant might be retained to prepare feasibility studies, design and implement market strategies, analyze investment portfolios, prepare site selection studies, provide counsel in price or lease negotiations, or offer litigation counsel.

The professional counselor's primary responsibility is to analyze all available alternatives and the probable consequences of each alternative and then to make recommendations that will enable the client to make the most beneficial decision.

Professional appraisers and counselors are retained on a fee basis, but neither employment nor the fee is contingent on the value or the recommendations. Accordingly, these professionals do not serve as advocates for any cause or faction. This should not be construed to suggest, however, that a counselor is forbidden to provide advice which is beneficial to the client.

The counselor may serve professionally in a position of advocacy in such matters as arbitration or negotiation on behalf of a client, but not on a contingent fee basis.

The dual appearance of an appraiser as a witness and as a counselor to lawyers examining other appraisal witnesses in the same proceeding is generally considered unprofessional. The appraiser or counselor might be of substantial assistance to the trial proceeding but should serve in only one capacity to avoid any implication of advocacy as to value conclusions.

Appraisers are customarily retained to express a value opinion as of a specific date and may be required to testify before a committee or court of law. The professional will not be influenced in the value conclusion by the owner, the client, or the circumstances, but will always reflect unbiased market observations.

Controversies of Definition and Concept

Frequently, divergent value opinions occur because of: 1) different interpretations of value definitions with inherent assumptions or implications, 2) misunderstanding of the economic principles affecting land and improvements, 3) failure to recognize fully the effects of zoning on economic use or value, or 4) use of varying client instructions as to assumptions.

The four essays in this section analyze the intricacies of the definition of market value and the principle of highest and best use. Determination of highest and best use is crucial to the estimation of market value and casual treatment will usually produce a weak and insupportable value estimate.

The structure of the prevailing definition of market value is confusing and its components are addressed separately as each is subject to various interpretations. These interpretations are controversial and frequently lead to value divergencies.

This section deals primarily with concepts and theory and essentially sets the stage for the examination of value approaches, methods, and techniques, which will be presented in Section 2.

A Critique of the Prevailing Definition of Market Value

INTRODUCTION

There are numerous points of controversy among appraisers regarding the definition of market value. The purpose of this essay is to analyze certain intricacies and suggest minor modifications in the market value definition that is typically cited by contemporary real property appraisers.

At least part of the problem can be attributed to the design and structure of the prevailing definition of market value, which often is misinterpreted by appraisers. The following comments are meant to provoke intelligent thought and additional research, which might lead to a better comprehension of the definition of market value and its proper application in the appraisal process.

MARKET VALUE DEFINED

The prevailing definition of market value evolved through a series of definitions which were acceptable in the various courts of the land. In more recent years, appraisers have modified these definitions to reflect contemporary problems and the possibility of alternative applications to reflect various market phenomena. One of the earlier definitions of market value accepted by appraisers stated:

> As defined by the courts, market value is the highest price estimated in terms of money which a property will bring if exposed for sale in the open market, allowing a reasonable time to find a purchaser who

This essay originally was published in the April 1980 issue of *The Appraisal Journal*.

buys with knowledge of all the uses to which it is adapted and for which it is capable of being used.[1]

The definition of market value in *Real Estate Appraisal Terminology,* sponsored jointly by the American Institute of Real Estate Appraisers and the Society of Real Estate Appraisers and published in 1975, has been accepted by most contemporary real property appraisers:

> MARKET VALUE. The highest price in terms of money which a property will bring in a competitive and open market under all conditions requisite to a fair sale, the buyer and seller, each acting prudently, knowledgeably and assuming the price is not affected by undue stimulus.
> Implicit in this definition is the consummation of a sale as of a specified date and the passing of title from seller to buyer under conditions whereby:
> 1. buyer and seller are typically motivated.
> 2. both parties are well informed or well advised, and each acting in what he considers his own best interest.
> 3. a reasonable time is allowed for exposure in the open market.
> 4. payment is made in cash or its equivalent.
> 5. financing, if any, is on terms generally available in the community at the specified date and typical for the property type in its locale.
> 6. the price represents a normal consideration for the property sold unaffected by special financing amounts and/or terms, services, fees, costs, or credits incurred in the transaction.

TOPICAL ANALYSIS

The preceding definition of market value involves many diverse elements of possible controversy, and parts of the definition, according to the significance attributed to certain phrases or concepts, have been subjectively selected for analysis.

"Highest Price"[2]

The term *highest price* has been the subject of substantial controversy in the courts, between appraisers and clients and among fellow appraisers, for

---

1. This definition, published in *Appraisal Terminology and Handbook* by the American Institute of Real Estate Appraisers in 1950, was derived essentially from *Sacramento Railroad Company* vs. *Heilbron,* 156 Calif 408(1909), p. 409.

2. Portions of this section were abstracted from an article by this author, entitled "Market Value—Highest Price or Most Probable Price?" published in "Notes and Comments" in *The Appraisal Journal,* July 1979.

many years. It appears that there can be no unanimity of opinion regarding the true meaning of the entire market value definition as previously presented.

Literal interpretation of highest price is judged to be no more logical than estimating lowest price and labeling it *market value*. The appraiser typically seeks to estimate fair market value, and the estimation of highest or lowest price would be unfair and not market value at all.

The professional appraiser is charged with the responsibility of estimating the most likely, most probable, or most reasonable price to buyer and seller, under conditions prevailing in the open market as of the date of the appraisal.

In reality, buyers and sellers conclude a final sale price after considerable negotiations beginning with an asking price that is higher or an offering price that is lower than the ultimate contract price. The final price reflects certain requirements of the buyer and seller; it is influenced by the negotiating skills of the parties and their agents as well as their respective motivations in consummating the deal. Most buyers are willing to pay more than the original offer and often might have agreed to pay more than the contract price. Likewise, most sellers ask for more and often might have agreed to accept less than the contract price.

The significance of these observations is that *price* is partially the result of varying degrees of negotiation skill. This negotiated price is not necessarily the highest price; it might be the lowest or highest price and could be somewhere between these extremes.

Where, then, did this highest price concept come from and what is implied by the use of the classic definition? The definition reflecting highest price is satisfactory but doesn't literally mean the most the property will bring in the market on the appraisal date.

A prudent investor typically views the prospective investment with consideration of all the reasonable alternatives of use or development. The alternative use that produces the highest net return or profit over a sustained period of time would produce the highest value and, therefore, theoretically represents the highest and best use of the property at that time. Accordingly, the highest price the prudent investor is willing to pay reflects the present worth of all future benefits of the property at optimum use to that investor.

The classic definition of market value, which is cited by most appraisers, doesn't mean highest price in a literal sense, but the most probable price at the highest and best use. This is consistent with the observation that the market value estimate would be the highest value reflected by detailed analyses of all logical potential use and development alternatives.[3]

"Terms of Money"

This phrase relates value to a medium of exchange, i.e., money, which might be expressed in dollars, pesos, yen, or some other currency. Many individuals believe that this phrase implies or confirms that market value must always be expressed in terms of anticipated cash transactions. In reality, many "markets" do not manifest themselves in terms of cash transactions. In such instances, the theory of cash equivalency as a substitute for market value is judged to be fallacious, as the following statements will attempt to show.

The "terms of money" part of the market value definition was apparently designed to eliminate the confusion which would be created if appraisers reported value conclusions in nonmonetary terms.

"Will Bring"

This part of the definition often has been misunderstood, because it implies that value is a fact. The property will bring a specific price, but it is the appraiser's task to estimate what the property should bring.

An appraisal is always an estimate and should not be construed as a scientific process resulting in a totally predictable price. Therefore, market value is an estimate of the price which a property should bring.

"Specified Date"

Market value is an estimate of the price at which the property should sell on the specific appraisal date and must be a present date or one in the past. It is inconceivable that market value can be professionally expressed as of a future date, because the estimate is the appraiser's reaction to market observations. The appraiser cannot express a supportable market value estimate relative to some date in the future, primarily because future market attitudes have not yet been established and economic conditions may change dramatically in the interim. Estimates of reversionary value for use in mortgage-equity analyses are not termed market value, because these esti-

---

3. It is noted that the 1981 edition of *Real Estate Appraisal Terminology* reflects the "most probable price . . . a property should bring" instead of the "highest price . . . a property will bring." This more recent definition is quite acceptable, accurate, and less confusing.

mates are not market-supported. Such estimates are anticipated collections and may well reflect substantially reduced purchasing power.

Appraisers who are inclined to speculate on future markets should be very careful to qualify an opinion as *probable future value, speculative value, stabilized value, retail value,* or some more descriptive term.

The market value definition presumes that a theoretical contract of sale and transfer, in terms of money at present purchasing power, will occur on the appraisal date. Obviously, such a transaction would be unusual and would not satisfy other parts of the definition, but the theory appears logical and practical.

"Reasonable Exposure" Required

The appraiser of market value obviously should analyze the existing market for the specific property type, as well as any anticipated market changes during the reasonable future.

Controversy arises over the question of whether the market value definition presumes that reasonable exposure in the market begins on the appraisal date or has already occurred in theory on that date.

This question becomes a great concern when the subject of the appraisal is a specialized manufacturing facility, large resort, or other "limited-market" property which may require one or more years to find a qualified purchaser. The extended time period might be necessary to establish marketing staffs, coordinate advertising, and expose the property to regional, national, or international prospects. Conversely, a four-unit residential property typically might sell in a local market within 30-90 days of market exposure with adequate promotion by experienced brokers.

In either event, the question remains an item of controversy. Value, the present worth of future benefits, is expressed as of the appraisal date. This reasonably implies that adequate and proper market exposure has occurred previously and that those marketing efforts should produce a price approximating the estimated market value, in terms of the specified monetary unit with present purchasing power, on the appraisal date.

If the converse theory is accepted, the appraiser effectively would be projecting values into the future and improperly labeling the estimate as present market value. This is erroneous, because collections of sales proceeds at any future date most likely will experience reduced purchasing power and other risks and should be discounted to present worth.

This is not to argue that, as of the appraisal date, a price approximating market value would be unattainable without future exposure. The controversy relates to whether the ultimate price reflects present market value or probable price several weeks, months, or years hence.

It is the author's contention that any estimate of market value must presume theoretical exposure has occurred by the appraisal date. Otherwise, the value must be projected to some future date and labeled something other than market value. The latter approach is weakened by diverse uncertainties such as future supply and demand, income and expense levels, purchasing power risks, changing investor yield requirements, speculation on adequate market exposure requirements, and discount rates.

Form of Payment

Extreme controversy presently exists among many professional appraisers, theoreticians, economists, and others regarding the form of payment in consummating a transaction under the market value concept. The most contemporary definition of market value, which was cited earlier in this chapter, includes several implicit requirements, and Items 4 and 5 are of primary concern here.

These statements, as written, may appear to be mutually exclusive, but they are judged to have been given to provide the appraiser with wide flexibility in adapting the definition to any assignment requiring the estimation of market value.

Historically, market value has been estimated as the most likely price obtainable in the specific market on the specific appraisal date, with reference to all known transactions involving similar properties selling with typical terms and conditions. Depending on the specifics of the market, properties in certain markets typically have sold for cash, while similar properties in totally different markets might well have sold with liberal seller financing. In other market situations, most or all of the purchase price might typically have been provided by third-party lenders.

Appraisers should interpret the market; if the prevailing market reflects cash transactions, then the market value definition requires the value estimate to reflect a cash transaction. If the typical transaction in the specific market involves 10% equity investment at closing and seller financing for the balance of the purchase price for 25-30 years, with 5-10 years of interest-only payments and amortization over the remaining mortgage term, these terms should be reflected in the appraiser's estimate of market value. Further discounting to cash equivalency and labeling it market value would be erroneous in this instance because it is inconsistent and not reflective of the market.

This is not to imply that cash equivalency has no import; it can be used advantageously and properly to: 1) "equalize" sales transactions involving diverse financing terms for data analysis purposes, 2) estimate cash market value, 3) counsel clients in structuring a range for the justifiable price, dependent on varying terms, or 4) counsel condemnors in negotiating acquisition prices for cash when sales of typical properties in that market usually are highly leveraged with seller financing.

The market value definition implicitly presumes passing of title under conditions whereby (as described under Items 4 and 5) payment is made in cash or its equivalent and financing, if any, is on terms generally available in the market. These literal statements appear reasonable, but are not mutually exclusive. This author interprets them to mean that "any" payment will be made in cash or its equivalent, with "equivalent" meaning that it is readily convertible to cash. Item 5, however, suggests that there well might be available financing and states that this financing, if any, is on terms generally available.

Some may argue that Item 5 relates to third-party financing and that all market value estimates still should be expressed in terms of Item 4, which, in essence, is cash equivalency. Others may argue that Item 6, relative to "special financing amounts and/or terms," supports Items 4 and 5. Item 6 is judged to relate to situations involving inordinate financing ratios and, perhaps, very low interest rates for extremely long mortgage terms, as offered by many lenders who had previously foreclosed on these properties. Those endorsing these arguments should review the basic definition of market value in its pure sense:

> The highest price in terms of money which a property will bring in a competitive and open market under all conditions requisite to a fair sale, the buyer and seller each acting prudently, knowledgeably and assuming the price is not affected by undue stimulus.

This is essentially the definition that professional appraisers accepted for many years before it was modernized into confusion. The basic or original definition is reasonably pure and comprehensible and doesn't restrict market value to all cash, all financing, or other appraiser-imposed peculiarities. The definition was meant to function within the market and, specifically, to enable appraisers to observe market phenomena and reflect those specific observations in the succeeding estimate of market value.

CONCLUSIONS

The basic definition is practicable, logical, and usable in all situations involving market value estimation, but minor changes in the presently accepted basic definition and one of the six modifier statements are recommended for adoption by professional appraisers.

A more comprehensible definition, developed by minor changes in the currently prevailing definition of market value, is recommended and would read as follows:

> Market value is defined as the *estimated* price, in terms of money, which a property *should bring* in a competitive and open market under all conditions requisite to a fair sale, with the buyer and seller each acting prudently and knowledgeably and presuming the price is not affected by undue influence.
>
> Implicit in this definition is the consummation of a sale as of a specified date and the passing of title from seller to buyer under conditions whereby:
> 1. Buyer and seller are typically motivated.
> 2. Both parties are well informed and well advised, acting in what they consider their own best interests.
> 3. A reasonable time is allowed for exposure in the open market.
> 4. *Equity* payment is made in cash or its equivalent.
> 5. Financing, if any, is on terms generally available in the community at the specified date and typical for the property type in its locale.
> 6. The price represents a normal consideration for the property sold, unaffected by special financing amounts and/or terms, services, fees, costs, or credits incurred in the transaction.

The six conditions are meaningful modifiers, but appraisers should be most careful not to lose sight of the primary objective of reflecting the specific and usually definable market. In those instances where the market is limited or nonexistent, the appraiser should have total flexibility to estimate or project terms of sale which will most likely be required or reflected upon sale at the estimated market value.

To ensure against further confusion, the appraisal report should be explicit regarding probable financing terms, particularly when seller financing is prevalent in a given market.

Distinction Between Price and Value

Substantial controversy exists among real estate salespeople, lenders, buyers, sellers, and appraisers regarding the commonly used terms *price* and *value*.

Salespeople are sometimes confronted with this problem when listing a property, because the seller may have unreasonable expectations of the property's potential. It is understandable that the seller desires the maximum price obtainable, but a misconception of value might affect the listing price and dampen market receptivity if the listed price is excessive. Buyers are also conscious of the vagaries of the market, and typically offer a contract at a low price to test the seller's motivation and desire to sell.

Value might well be different to the buyer and seller of the same property. The ultimate contract price is usually established after considerable negotiation, and most buyers and sellers believe that the executed contract is more advantageous to their respective positions. The typical buyer would likely have been willing to pay more, while the typical seller would likely have been willing to accept less. Salespeople are usually aware that prices are dependent on negotiation skills, the dissimilar motives of buyer and seller, and the ability of the property to satisfy the specific needs of the buyer.

Lenders are usually very concerned with value, as most institutional lenders and commercial banks are restricted against lending more than some specified percent of value or price, whichever is lower. If the sales

Reprinted from the February 1980 issue of *real estate today*® by permission of the National Association of REALTORS® and the REALTORS National Marketing Institute® of the National Association of REALTORS®.

15

contract is conditioned on the purchaser obtaining a loan for a determinable period and interest rate and for 75% of the price, and the typical lender would be willing to issue a loan of 75% of appraised value, all parties would be concerned with the possibility that value and price might differ.

The salesperson would hope that value is at least as great as price so that the sale can be consummated. The seller and buyer would likely hope that price and value are equal in the eyes of the lender, although they might well have private opinions of the differences. Although the lender is usually protected by the amount of equity invested by the borrower, a loan based on a liberal value could have significant financial and legal effects on the lender.

Appraisers are often retained by buyers, sellers, developers, salespeople, lenders, or others for counsel in contract negotiations or to provide value estimates for other reasons. When two or more parties disagree, the appraiser might be under extreme pressure to estimate a preconceived value.

The professional appraiser is often criticized for being too conservative, particularly if the appraisal reflects a value estimate which is less than the contract price. For this reason, the following comments are offered with the sincere desire to minimize future controversy in these matters.

The monetary sum paid for real property is customarily reported as price and represents a fact. Conversely, value is always expressed as an opinion or estimate. Real estate practitioners are familiar with other terms such as asking price, listed price, and offered price, but these are qualified terms and not prices at all.

Value is a word with diverse applications and is subject to misinterpretation. Value is basically a relationship between a person and the object desired. The value of a pitcher of water to one who is dehydrated would be greater than the value of a second pitcher of water to the same person at essentially the same time.

Value may be defined generally as the estimated present worth of future benefits. The value of a home to a particular owner or buyer would essentially be the sum of the present worth of the rights of use—the anticipated joy of ownership, tax advantages of ownership, and the prospects of equity growth through debt amortization and increasing prices. In this context, value relates the property to a specific owner or user.

It is significant to note that value in the general sense differs among individuals, as is evidenced by varying prices paid for virtually identical properties in the same market area.

Sale price reflects the value relationship established between a buyer and a seller for a property on a specific date. It can hardly be argued that price conclusively establishes value if the market reflects sales of other, similar properties at different prices at approximately the same date. One sale does not usually establish the market, but several sales of similar properties can be strong indicators of diverse market attitudes and reflect a range of probable value for use by the agent or appraiser.

If prices reflect the value to specific buyers and the properties are similar in most physical, locational, and economic characteristics, it would appear that there is a major inconsistency between price and value when prices vary substantially. This inconsistency can be clarified by further explanation of the true meaning of value. The professional appraiser is typically retained to estimate "market value," which was discussed in great detail in the preceding chapter.

In addition to market value, many other types of value may be estimated by qualified appraisers and analysts. These are discussed briefly here to emphasize that the generic term, *value,* should be used with caution.

1. *Cash equivalent value* is the market value discounted to reflect cash terms, if the prevailing market is one which reflects liberal seller financing.
2. *Insurable value* is the value of the improvements for insurance purposes. This has no relationship to market conditions or economics.
3. *Liquidation value* is the anticipated price obtainable at auction or upon immediate sale without normal marketing efforts.
4. *Assessed value* is the value used by tax assessors for calculating ad valorem taxes. This may or may not relate to market value in the true sense of the market and economics, although assessors usually compute assessed value as a percentage of their estimate of market value.
5. *Value in use* is the value to a specific user. This typically relates to a limited-market or special-use property such as a manufacturing plant, church, school, or library.
6. *Investment value* is the value of a particular investment property to an investor with consideration given to the tax bracket and investor yield requirements of that investor. Investment value has no relationship to market conditions or general economics.
7. *Stabilized value* is the market value of the property on the appraisal date, predicated on the assumption that the property has attained stabilization of occupancy, rental rates, and operating expenses.

8. *Speculative value* is the estimated price a speculator would be justified in paying for a property which has no development or use potential in the immediate future. This type of value might be sought in advising a buyer on purchasing land in an inactive market. It would typically require discounting some expected future value to reflect the uncertainties of time and the costs to carry.

For most market value appraisal assignments, appraisers analyze prices of similar properties to abstract value indicators.

The appraiser or analyst might be employed to provide advice or assistance in matters not involving market value. In those instances, the report may not be based on actual market observations, but should be qualified to eliminate any questions about the type of value estimated.

Distinction Among Appraisals, Marketability Studies, and Feasibility Studies

Most people familiar with real estate activities recognize that an appraisal is an estimate of value, but many mistakenly assume that *marketability studies* and *feasibility studies* are synonymous. Every appraisal of market value should be based on some reasonable semblance of marketability and feasibility analyses. Substituting one term for the other frequently implies project feasibility, which might be erroneous and could result in value divergencies or unwise investment decisions.

MARKETABILITY STUDY

A properly executed marketability study will include an exhaustive search for economic data from which the analyst will derive reasonable conclusions about the marketability of the product. Accurate determination of the project's market and marketability will have significant impact on the financial profitability, or feasibility, of the venture. The estimate of market value will usually depend on the appraiser's confidence in the projections regarding marketability and feasibility.

Frequently, appraisers are requested to prepare appraisals of real property that is essentially only an idea or, perhaps, a finite plan. In many instances, marketability and feasibility considerations are of greater significance to the client than the value estimate.

The marketability study is an attempt to define the market and the specific products that will best satisfy the demands of the market at that time or in the near future. The market study should reveal the type and size of units that are most marketable and reveal the probable rent or price range.

19

It will also provide insights into the market's historical absorption, which should prove most helpful in projecting absorption rates at those price levels.

It would be unwise to retain a land planner or architect to design plans for construction unless the developer is totally aware of the market potential for the product. For example, a project designed to include three- and four-bedroom condominium units in a resort area where the market is for smaller one- and two-bedroom units might be absorbed slowly and at prices below the expectancy of the developer. This single factor could dramatically affect the financial feasibility of the project.

FEASIBILITY STUDY

A feasibility study is basically an analysis of the economics of a specific project to determine whether it should be developed. The ultimate decision should rest on the determination of the project's financial profitability. If the market value of the project is less than or equal to its cost, it is usually obvious that the project is not financially feasible unless development modifications are implemented.

Financial feasibility is evident in most instances where the market value exceeds total cost plus a margin of entrepreneurial profit deemed sufficient to attract the equity "risk" capital of prudent investors. The analyst should include the value of the land, not necessarily its cost if purchased several years before, as land investment. Otherwise, the feasibility conclusions could be distorted as the margin of profitability could be reflected by the land increment.

A method to test the financial feasibility of two income/investment properties follows:

Project A. Office Building Renovation

1. Value upon Renovation

Gross rent potential	
(20,000 sq. ft. @ $11.00)	$220,000
Less vacancy and collection loss allowance (5%)	11,000
Effective gross annual income	$209,000
Less fixed and operating expenses	
(20,000 sq.ft. @ $5.50)	110,000
Net income before debt service	$ 99,000
Market value indicated by capitalization	
($99,000 ÷ .095 overall rate)	$1,042,000

2. Feasibility Analysis/Test

Deduct

Cost or value of land and improvements before renovation	$450,000	
Direct renovation costs	150,000	
Indirect expenses (interest, insurance, utilities, and taxes during renovation; architectural and engineering fees; and projected rent loss during one year lease/occupancy period)	200,000	800,000
Margin of entrepreneurial profit		$ 242,000
Indicated profit rate ($242,000 ÷ $800,000)		30.25%

Project B. New Warehouse Construction

1. Value upon Completion

Gross rent potential—per lease (15,000 sq. ft. @ $1.50)	$22,500
Less vacancy and collection loss allowance (None—leased to AAA national company)	-0-
Effective gross annual income	$22,500
Less fixed and operating expenses (15,000 sq. ft. @ $.50)	7,500
Net income before debt service	$15,000
Market value indicated by capitalization ($15,000 ÷ .09 overall rate)	$167,000

2. Feasibility Analysis/Test

Deduct

Turnkey construction contract (including site)	$150,000	
Indirect costs (interest, insurance, and taxes during construction; architectural and engineering fees)	30,000	180,000
Margin of entrepreneurial profit (loss)		($ 13,000)
Indicated profit (loss) rate ($13,000 ÷ $180,000)		(7.22%)

In the preceding examples, Project A is clearly feasible from an entrepreneurial perspective, before analysis of tax consequences; Project B is clearly not financially feasible. The feasibility decision would be more difficult where the indicated margin of profit equals or slightly exceeds the total investment cost. In such instances, the feasibility analyst would be justified in recommending against acquisition, renovation, or construction if the prospective margin of profit is less than a predetermined amount or percentage of acquisition, renovation, or construction costs.

In the examples, the margin of profit or loss is related to total investment costs. It may be customary or desirable to relate profitability to total value upon completion of the proposed project. When analyzing various investment alternatives, it is wise to use caution to ensure that all feasibility studies are consistently analyzed with regard to the measurement of profit margins and rates.

Note that the appraiser performs a valuation service when a value estimate is derived from market analysis/observation. Market studies comprise a major part of the appraisal, but it is not uncommon for an appraiser/analyst to perform a market study that will not be used in an appraisal study. Such market studies, as well as feasibility studies, are generally considered to be nonappraisal evaluation or consultation services, although they may be prepared by qualified, experienced real property appraisers.

Highest and Best Use Considerations

Because value is defined as the present worth of future benefits, most prudent realty investors and owners probably would agree that price reflects investor observations and understanding regarding the potential of the property during the probable ownership period. Price normally would be established by negotiations between two or more parties who presumably are aware of economic conditions existing in the specific market at that time.

The definition of market value is always predicated on the presumption that the appraiser has accurately analyzed all relevant economic factors and made reasonable determinations as to the highest and best use of the real property at that date. The validity of the market value estimate is directly related to the confidence in the appraiser's conclusion regarding highest and best use.

Highest and best use is the logical, legal, and most probable use that will produce the highest net return to the investor over a sustained period of time. It is also the available use or program of probable future utilization that produces the highest present land value.

DETERMINING HIGHEST AND BEST USE

In analyzing the highest and best use of any property, all use or development alternatives must be considered in light of: 1) legal factors such as zoning and building codes, 2) logic, and 3) productivity or profitability.

Portions of this essay originally appeared under the title, "Testing Highest and Best Use," in the July 1979 issue of *The Appraisal Journal*.

The optimum use of land that is zoned for apartments may be single-family residential subdivision development. Commercially zoned land might have greater productivity for office, apartment, or single-family subdivision development. The productivity of a hotel building may be increased by its conversion to housing for the elderly, apartments, condominiums, or modernization for continued hotel usage. The highest and best use of rental apartments might be condominium residences or offices.

A detailed market study and economic analysis often suggest that greater profitability can be realized by combining apartment units to create larger, more marketable units, or vice versa. A thorough analysis might reveal that a different mix of unit types would be more salable, more efficient, and more profitable to the typical, prudent investor.

Detailed highest and best use analyses are not applicable in all circumstances. If there is no prevalent use or manifest demand for development, the highest and best use of a site or tract might be for speculative holding. If buildings represent a minor economic part of the total property value, the "taxpayer" status of the improvements represents the interim use while the investor decides how and when to redevelop the site. This subject will be discussed later in this chapter.

In analyzing possible uses, consideration must be given to market demands, supply, attitudinal changes of consumers, growth and development patterns, and other trends. Profitability is influenced by the duration of marketing periods and concomitant holding costs such as ad valorem taxes, insurance, management expenses, and the costs of maintenance. The prudent investor/developer will also recognize probable costs of sales and entrepreneurial risks that affect prospects for entrepreneurial profit. A margin of profit adequate to attract an investor into a development or conversion project must be considered in determining financial feasibility before reaching a conclusion of highest and best use.

TESTING FOR VALIDITY OF HIGHEST AND BEST USE

In all analyses of highest and best use, the legal permissibility, logic, and profitability or probability of the development must be tested.

The economy of the area may indicate a demand for additional apartments. Present zoning may preclude apartments, however, and the politics of the jurisdiction could be unfavorable for zoning changes or variances. Private deed restrictions or neighborhood association agreements also may preclude specific developments even though economics dictate otherwise.

Market factors may suggest a need for a large office building in the area, even though the site being analyzed is in the middle of a modern single-family subdivision. Accordingly, office development probably would not be logical even if legally permissible.

Development of housing for the elderly might be permissible for a specific site, but if most residents of the area are under 40 years of age such development would not be logical and probably would not satisfy the requirement of profitability.

Determining the highest and best use of vacant sites and improved properties requires detailed analyses of all reasonable development or use alternatives. For the sake of simplicity, a vacant site is evaluated here to ascertain its highest and best use. The principles of testing the optimum use of developed building sites are essentially the same as those used in the analysis of vacant sites.

DETERMINING CONSTRUCTION FOR OPTIMUM SITE USE

Presume that the rectangular subject lot has dimensions of 100 feet by 200 feet, contains 20,000 square feet of land area, and is zoned commercial. Research reveals that there is a high occupancy rate in residences, apartments, retail space, offices, and other similar uses throughout the area. The commercial zoning permits all of these uses. Research and analysis of numerous land sales lead the appraiser to conclude that the vacant site has a present market value of $30,000.

What development will maximize the potential of the site—perhaps a residence, apartment project, office building, retail center, hotel/motel, or service station?

Residence Project

Presume that the typical residence that would be marketable at this location would contain 1,100 square feet and cost $25,000 to construct. Additional market research reveals that upon completion this typical residence and site would likely sell for $40,000. The economics of this development or use alternative are summarized:

Reproduction cost new	$25,000
Land value estimate	+ 30,000
Total investment required	$55,000
Less anticipated sale price	−40,000
Anticipated profit (loss)	($15,000)

The developer would have invested time and effort in construction co-ordination, been exposed to other entrepreneurial risks, and invested money or personal time in marketing the property, which theoretically would produce an even greater loss. Obviously, a prudent developer or owner of this site would not consider this development program.

Apartment Project

The site is large enough to permit only 10 units under the present zoning. Market research indicates that there is no real demand for one- or four-bedroom units and that 60% of the units constructed for this market should have two bedrooms, and 40% should have three bedrooms. We also could determine the most marketable price of the two- and three-bedroom units and conclude that they should rent readily for $150 and $200 per month, respectively. A projected cost of constructing the apartment improvements is $170,000; therefore, the total investment in buildings and land would approximate $200,000.

The appraiser recognizes that probably not all scheduled rents would be collected throughout the typical ownership period because some tenants may default, and units are not always occupied by new tenants on the same day previous tenants vacate.

The economics of the hypothetical apartment project are summarized:

Annual market rent potential:	
6 units @ $150 × 12 mos.	$10,800
4 units @ $200 × 12 mos.	9,600
Gross potential rental income	$20,400
Less vacancy and collection loss	
allowance (5%)	1,000
Effective gross income	$19,400
Less estimated expenses and	
replacement reserves	7,400
Estimated net operating income	
before debt service	$12,000

The $12,000 net operating income reflects only a 6% annual return on the total $200,000 investment in land and buildings. Presume market analyses reveal that similar apartment properties and other similar investment alternatives have sold recently to produce overall rates of return of 9.5%—10.5% annually. Accordingly, the hypothetical apartment example is economically infeasible.

Another method of analysis is to allocate net operating income first to satisfy the investment in land at, say, 9% annually, with the residual allocated to the cost of improvements, which should earn at, say, 12% annually. Therefore,

Net operating income estimate	$12,000
Less land requirements	
($30,000 value @ 9%)	2,700
Income residual to improvements	$9,300

The improvements costing $170,000 should earn $20,400 per year ($170,000 @ 12%); but only $9,300 in net income is available for the improvements. Accordingly, the $11,100 theoretical deficit strongly confirms that the apartments would not be an economically feasible development and should not be considered further.

Similar analyses should be made for other alternative development programs. Presume that all possible uses except a small office building have been properly analyzed and eliminated from further consideration.

Office Building Project

Market investigation reveals that a market does exist for office space, which should rent at $5 per square foot of rentable area per year inclusive of all building services and utilities except telephone.

We must determine how large the office building should be. The zoning ordinance specifies that only 40% of the commercially zoned site can be covered by building, unless a parking deck is provided on the site. A deck is projected to cost $6 per square foot to construct. Land value is $1.50 per square foot ($30,000 ÷ 20,000 square feet). Therefore, if the necessary land is convenient and available, building a deck would not be wise.

The zoning ordinance further stipulates that the maximum permissible building height is 50 feet, or four stories. The maximum gross building area may be calculated:

20,000 sq. ft. site × .40 × 4 floors = 32,000 sq. ft.

Leasable area, at 80% building efficiency, is calculated at 25,600 square feet. With 40% site coverage, a total of 12,000 square feet of land area would be available for on-site parking. If typical parking spaces, including drives, contain approximately 300 square feet on surface lots, a maximum of 40 spaces or 1.6 spaces per 1,000 square feet of gross leasable area would be provided. If this is insufficient parking, the analyst should consider possible land assemblage or construction of a parking deck.

In analyzing the office building as a possible development alternative, the improvement cost is projected at $600,000, and a 40-year economic life is considered reasonable. A 9% annual risk rate is believed reasonable for land and improvements, and the investment in improvements is projected for recovery by annual installments of the building net income into a sinking fund earning at the 9% risk rate, to enable full recovery of the investment by the end of the 40th year. The process is summarized:

Gross annual income potential	
(25,600 sq. ft. @ $5)	$128,000
Less vacancy, expense, and reserve estimates	51,000
Estimated net operating income	
before debt service	$77,000
Less annual building requirement at 9%	
risk rate ($600,000 × .09296)	55,775
Net annual income residual to land	$21,225

The implied land value, by capitalization at 9%, is approximately $235,000, which strongly suggests that this office project is financially feasible. This capitalization technique is based on the presumption of a constant net income throughout the economic life. Use of all other capitalization techniques confirms that the capitalized or implied land value under this development alternative substantially exceeds the $30,000 market value estimated for the land by market comparison. Therefore, the office use is logical, legal, and the most profitable of all reasonable alternatives; it represents a highest and best use of the site.

These analyses should not be construed as true indicators of land value, but only as indicators of the project's financial feasibility. Land value is established at $30,000, and the $235,000 land value implied by the office analysis actually includes a fair value of the land and a $205,000 premium, 33% above the projected construction cost of the office improvements.

ADDITIONAL CONSIDERATIONS

Additional questions should be considered before a final conclusion is reached. Would the office space rent for more if additional on-site parking were provided? How much more? Should the proposed building size be reduced to accommodate more parking per square foot of leasable area? After testing the alternatives, a specific type and size building should be recommended for the site.

The preceding processes also can be used to determine the maximum justifiable investment in land and improvements, recognizing the economics of the area and site.

Although ascertaining the optimum use of a vacant site has been the primary purpose of this discussion so far, these processes can also be used in analyzing the potential for modernizing or converting improved properties to alternative uses. To increase the probability that an investment will be financially feasible for at least the anticipated ownership period, all economic principles should be analyzed carefully.

INTERIM USE VALUE OF IMPROVEMENTS

As mentioned earlier, if the existing improvements represent only a small part of the property's total value, but there is no immediate demand for redevelopment, the present improvements may represent an interim use until it is feasible to develop the site to its highest and best use. In fact, most existing improvements include substantial obsolescence, including superadequacies, deficiencies, or improper location on the site. Accordingly, prudent ownership would not reconstruct identical buildings on the site if it were vacant and available for redevelopment. Therefore, it appears that most improvements do not develop sites to their respective optimum uses.

For example, a building and its site might have an estimated market value of $100,000. If the land, presumed to be vacant, has a market value of $80,000, the improvements have an implied value of $20,000. If prudent ownership expects to develop the typical site to reflect a 1:4 land-to-building investment ratio, it is apparent that this building does not develop the site to its highest and best use. Prudent ownership would not raze the improvements to create a vacant site worth $80,000, however, so the present highest and best use of the property package is continued use as committed. This does not preclude economic conversion to an alternative use which might improve the profitability of the overall property.

Development of a site to its optimum use seldom occurs because the definition of highest and best use demands a proper balance of all units in production relative to the property. This may occur at the time of original construction, but many newly constructed facilities fail to meet the test. The principle of highest and best use is of great significance in the relational analyses within the various valuation approaches. A functional building, completed yesterday, may have exquisite finish and quality workmanship and yet have no economic value. The actual or estimated construction cost has no effect on the market value estimate.

A recently completed office project has an estimated market value, as developed, of $1,100,000. However, the site has a present worth of $1,250,000 if vacant. Therefore, the building and related improvements have no economic value although they were recently constructed at a cost of $1,000,000.

Analyses of highest and best use are processes designed to test the ability of available or potential net operating income to satisfy the investment in land. If the income cannot satisfy the land requirement, the improvements are typically judged to have no economic value and do not develop the site to its optimum use. In such instances, the cost of razing the improvements is typically deducted from the estimated land value if vacant to derive a market value estimate as developed. This process is proper if the subject property is compared with market data involving vacant sites. If the market data shows that sites with improvements have no economic value, the subject value conclusion does not require further adjustment for anticipated demolition costs or the interim-use value of improvements because the subject and comparable sites are similar in that respect.

Writing in 1978, Robert L. Blake clearly demonstrated that "there are situations where interim-income value may be added to land value" instead of deducting for demolition costs.[1] A vacant site is invariably worth more than a site with obsolete improvements, presuming the site is economically ripe for redevelopment and demolition costs exceed the salvage value of the improvements. If the site is not likely to be developed in the immediate future, a prudent investor might rather own a site with existing improvements than a vacant site, presuming the improvements are capable of reducing the net cash losses during the interim period before anticipated redevelopment.

Blake illustrates interim-use valuation with two examples, assuming that salvage value will equal demolition cost. In one example, land value is clearly documented at $100,000 by recent sales of similar commercial sites. The subject site and improvements are capable of producing $3,600 per year for the anticipated ten years prior to redevelopment. The site, if vacant, would produce no revenue, and taxes would be $900 per year. As improved, total annual expenses for insurance, maintenance, and taxes—including those on improvements—are approximately $2,000; thus, net operating income is $1,600 per year.

A fair return on the land, if vacant, is estimated to be 8% of value, or $8,000. It is evident that the improvements do not develop the site to optimum use. However, the site is more desirable improved than vacant because the improved site has a positive net income of $1,600 per year, as opposed to a $900 net loss per year for the vacant site. The net advantage of

---

1. Robert L. Blake, "The Interim-Income Approach to Value of Improvements No Longer Suited to Highest and Best Use," *The Appraisal Journal,* October 1978, pp. 588-591.

the improved site is therefore $2,500 per year for the ten years before anticipated development.

If the risk rate is 12% per annum, the factor representing the present worth of the right to receive $1 per year for ten years is 5.65. Therefore, the improvements have an interim value of approximately $14,000 ($2,500 × 5.65 = $14,125). The indicated value of the property is $114,000, allocated $100,000 to land and $14,000 to improvements.

If the subject site has the capability of producing some net income if vacant, but more as developed, the net income difference would be multiplied by the present worth factor to derive an interim-use value of the improvements.

The appraiser of partial and total takings in eminent domain proceedings may be faced with several interesting circumstances, including:

1. Allocation of market value to the land and the improvements before and after the taking.
2. Possible reduction in the value of the remainder site and improvements in partial takings.
3. Possible remainder site appreciation and a corresponding decrease in the interim-use value of the improvements.
4. Possible remainder site depreciation and a corresponding increase in the value of improvements. This is somewhat a reversal of economic obsolescence affecting the improvements.
5. Possible acceleration of the development point for the remainder parcel and elimination of the interim-use value of improvements, thus effecting damages to the extent of improvement value in the instance of partial land taking.

CONCLUSIONS ON HIGHEST AND BEST USE DIVERGENCIES

Value divergencies frequently occur because appraisers disagree about the optimal use of the land if vacant, or the total property as improved.

An appraiser of a vacant site might conclude optimum use based on a physical site inspection, casually observing the physical surroundings or known subject zoning. Another appraiser might reach a conflicting conclusion after a similar limited observation or upon completing a more detailed market study and processing economic data. Appraisers who rely on observation of the committed use of improved sites and do not perform economic studies will frequently err in their conclusion of optimum use. The existing improvements may have substantial economic value, interim-use value, or no economic value at all; the latter conclusion suggests that immediate demolition would be prudent.

The appraiser's selection of the method for determining highest and best use will affect the type and magnitude of market data to be gathered. Limiting a data search to be consistent with observed physical and minimal economic conditions would exclude data which might suggest a totally different conclusion. Market value cannot be reasonably estimated and supported if the premise of optimum use is not reliable.

Zoning and Nonconforming Uses

Determining the optimum use and value of a site is partially dependent on the existing zoning classification or the probability of rezoning the site to permit a use consistent with its economic potential. The appraiser of improved real estate estimates the market value of the site at its highest and best use if vacant, and adds the contributory value of the improvements to derive a property value indication. It is critically important that the contributory value of the improvements reflects any obsolescence caused by inconsistencies between the existing use and the potential uses of the site.

In instances where the land is committed to a use which is legal and reasonably conforms to optimum use, the land value can usually be estimated with reasonable market support. Conversely, complex valuation problems may arise when the site is committed to a nonconforming, but legal, use.

Zoning ordinances typically provide that existing improvements may continue as legal uses without time constraints, but the site cannot be redeveloped and similar, nonconforming uses cannot be continued after the improvements are destroyed by disaster or voluntary removal. Most ordinances do not preclude remodeling to extend the improvements' economic lives, but conversion to alternative uses might trigger mandatory compliance.

The appraiser of a nonconforming property must decide whether to appraise the site as if it were vacant or as committed. In developed neighborhoods, market data on similar sites may be nonexistent and pertinent data on sales of lower-density sites might be difficult to compare with the subject site and its zoning.

The appraiser may elect not to appraise the site as if vacant, or to use the cost approach if the improvements are old and no recent land sales data are available. The cost approach might well be an unreliable value indicator. Land valuations would likely be necessary, however, when partial takings and easements are proposed, when component depreciation studies demand price/value allocations, and when "insurable value" estimates are sought.

UNDER/OVER DEVELOPED

Typical problems facing the appraiser of nonconforming property involve sites where: 1) a zoning variance enables greater development density, 2) the existing density substantially exceeds potential development densities, or 3) the existing development density is less than that permissible under current zoning regulations.

The improvements may not contribute value to the underdeveloped site, so it would be appraised as if vacant and the value possibly adjusted to deduct demolition costs. It would be improper to further penalize the value of the site for underdevelopment, primarily because of the principle of highest and best use as applicable to the site.

Valuation of the property and site poses substantially different problems if zoning allows greater density than developed or if density exceeds existing zoning. It is quite likely that a value premium would be ascribable to either the land or the improvements depending on the situation. Some may argue that any value premium is a result of the greater rentable area or number of units and cannot therefore be ascribable to the land. Others may contend that zoning controls land use and the premium applies to the land. Still others might argue that any value premium would expire with the existing improvements and this should be considered a temporary nonrealty, or intangible, license value.

Nomenclature is of little significance, but the appraiser should be deliberate and cautious. It is quite possible for a partial taking of a land area through eminent domain to detrimentally affect the remaining land and improvements and, perhaps, reduce the value of the "license." It is most important to ensure that the owner is financially unharmed.

CASE STUDY

Assume that a 10,000-sq.ft.(0.23-acre) site with 50 feet of street frontage is zoned to permit seven rental apartment units, but it is developed with 12 units. The legal, nonconforming use could have resulted from a zoning variance or development prior to the current ordinance. Data searches reveal no sales, listings, or leases of vacant sites considered similar and competitive with the subject site. Data pertaining to sales of similar improved properties in the area having similar zoning nonconformities were available for analysis.

Additional data searches revealed that vacant parcels, purchased for anticipated lower-density development in accordance with the current zoning ordinance, have recently sold at prices ranging from $1,700–$2,000 per permissible unit, or $30,600–$36,000 per acre. These data were gathered from sites that permit 18 dwelling units per acre. The subject site is developed to a density of 52 units per acre, and the current zoning permits 30 units per acre.

These data suggest value indications for the subject property:

Units permissible
$1,700 × 7 units = $11,900
$2,000 × 7 units = $14,000

Units constructed
$1,700 × 12 units = $20,400
$2,000 × 12 units = $24,000

Acreage
$30,600 × .23 acre = $7,038
$36,000 × .23 acre = $8,280

There is greater correlation between the land values indicated by analyses of permissible units and acreage because of the common criteria. The subject land value indicated for units constructed, however, is developed by extrapolation and reflects certain distortions. The sites from which these market data were developed reflect substantially lower densities. Therefore, these sites might be more desirable because of their development and aesthetic aspects. The sales prices per permissible unit might be greater because of the noncluttered design; thus, these sites might represent an upper limit of subject land value per constructed unit. On the other hand, the subject units could produce a greater rent due to their close-in, or prime, location, thus offsetting the aesthetic advantages of the lower-density development.

In practical application, a realistic preliminary conclusion from these data might indicate a subject land value in the range of $15,000–$20,000, or $1,250–$1,667 per existing unit. The final estimate of land value may be reserved until the entire subject property has been appraised using appropriate comparison and capitalization processes. The final land value

estimate might logically be allocated with consideration given to the preliminary land value estimate and the relationship of total property value
to preliminary land value.

VALUATION OF ZONING VARIANCE AND BUILDING PERMIT

The appraisal subject or a "comparable" sale may have a zoning variance and permit to construct more floors, more office space, or more
apartment units, or to develop residential lots with less frontage or land
area than permissible by the current zoning. Assessment of the effect of
this frequent occurrence involves analyzing the profitability of each of the
available alternatives. It is quite possible that the site with a variance to
construct "excess" space could have less implied value than if it were developed in accordance with the zoning ordinance.

Assume that the site is zoned to permit 100 dwelling units and the
market-supported land value is $2,000 per permissible unit, or $200,000.
The developer has obtained a variance and permit to construct 200 units.
Market research reveals that the units should be identical and cost $13,000
each, exclusive of land. Because of extremely high density, the unit rentals
in this market are likely to be less than the $300 monthly rentals which
could be expected if the site were developed in accordance with the current
zoning. Market analysis strongly supports the following range of market
rents for the alternative densities:

Alternative	No. of Units	Monthly Unit Rent
A	100	$300
B	125	300
C	150	275
D	175	265
E	200	250

The variance and permit will have value only if a larger project proves
more profitable after providing a fair return on the building costs under
each of the development alternatives. The net operating income before
debt service in each alternative is reasonably estimated at 50% of the gross
market rent potential. The required return on the building costs under
each alternative is computed with an annuity factor which provides for
10% annual return on investment plus annual recapture or return of the
costs over a 40-year period. The annuity factor for 10% interest and a 40-
year period is 0.1023. The accompanying table summarizes the apparent
economics of each development alternative.

	A	B	C	D	E
No. of units	100	125	150	175	200
Estimated cost (excluding land)	$1,300,000	$1,625,000	$1,950,000	$2,275,000	$2,600,000
Unit rent/month	300	300	275	265	250
Annual rent	360,000	450,000	495,000	556,500	600,000
Net income	180,000	225,000	247,500	278,250	300,000
Less annual return to improvements (cost × .1023)	132,990	166,238	199,485	232,733	265,980
Net to land	$ 47,010	$ 58,762	$ 48,015	$ 45,517	$ 34,020

It is evident that a prudent developer would not construct more than 125 units on the site, as residual land return is maximized at this density. The developer might perhaps rationalize a 150-unit development, but net income to land plummets for a project larger than 150 units. If the developer decides to build 125 units instead of the allowable 200 units, construction of the 25 "excess" units (over the 100 permitted by zoning without variance or permit) would produce a net premium of $11,752 per year ($58,762 − $47,010) to land for the anticipated economic life of the project.

The present worth of the right to receive $11,752 at the end of each year for 40 years, with discounting at 10% per year, is approximately $115,000 ($11,752 × present worth factor of 9.7791), which is the apparent value of the variance and permit allowing excess construction on the site. It would not be practical to capitalize the income into perpetuity as most variances apply to a specific use or a specific duration. It cannot be assumed that the variance would be renewed upon expiration of the economic life of the proposed improvements.

This analysis suggests a premium value of $115,000 for the right to construct up to 100 additional units, or $1,150 per unit. It should be noted, however, that only 25 additional units are economically justifiable; therefore, the premium value is effectively $4,600 per "excess" unit.

Before reaching a conclusion as to the plausibility of this apparent premium value, it should be recalled that the land value was earlier judged to be market-supported at $2,000 per unit, or $200,000 for the 100-unit site before consideration of the zoning variance. If the market expresses land price/value at $2,000 per unit, the imputed value of $4,600 per unit for the "excess" capacity is probably erroneous, particularly if there is a supply of land available for apartment development in the area.

An appraiser electing to utilize straight-line recapture instead of the annuity form should expect somewhat different numerical results, but perhaps the same practical decisions. The principal problem is that straight capitalization with straight-line recapture always presumes a declining net annual income at a constant, straight-line rate. This is probably illogical for most apartment projects, and particularly for new ones because apartment rents tend to escalate. Net income seldom declines on a systematic, straight-line basis.

For comparative analyses, the net income figures for the development alternatives previously discussed are summarized and calculated using straight-line recapture during a 40-year life (2.5% per year) with a 10% annual risk rate.

	A	B	C	D	E
No. of units	100	125	150	175	200
Net income	$180,000	$225,000	$247,500	$278,250	$300,000
Less annual return to improvements (cost × .125)	162,500	203,125	243,750	284,375	325,000
Net to land	$ 17,500	$ 21,875	$ 3,750	($ 6,125)	($ 25,000)

Note that alternatives D and E will not produce sufficient net incomes to satisfy building return requirements, and therefore no residuals are available for land.

The preceding analysis confirms that alternative B (with 125 units) maximizes the subject development. With this valuation premise, the construction of 25 additional units would produce a net premium of $4,375 per year ($21,875 − $17,500) to the land for the anticipated economic life of the project. The present worth of the right to receive $4,375 at the end of each year for 40 years, utilizing the 9.7791 present worth factor for 10% as previously selected, is computed: $4,375 × 9.7791 = $42,800. This value premium approximates $1,712 per additional dwelling unit constructed.

As the two valuation premises considered reflect substantially different value estimates for the zoning variance, the appraiser should take care to select the method and technique that best reflect the most likely reinvestment of recaptured funds. Although both recapture premises have merit, the annuity method is considered most plausible in the subject instance. It is more logical to presume that recaptured funds will be reinvested at the risk rate of 10%, than to presume straight-line recapture with recaptured funds not reinvested. Coupled with anticipated net income decline, the straight-line method/technique is not credible for the subject case.

Major Areas of Vulnerability in the Valuation Process

This section relates to the appraisal process, the valuation approaches, and several areas of particular vulnerability which frequently cause controversies and divergencies.

A short discussion of the appraisal process is presented as an introduction to the interrelationships of the sales comparison, income, and cost approaches, which are usually processed independently. Divergencies of opinion can occur at numerous points of vulnerability within the three value approaches and in the reconciliation process.

The discussion of "rules of thumb" in the appraisal process suggests that value opinions may differ because appraisers rely on certain common rules of thumb with little understanding of the factors that influence profitability, price, and value. Casual use of rules of thumb, capitalization rates, and expense ratios without realistic analysis of market transactions and operating statements involving similar properties can cause divergencies. A method for testing the reliability of estimated gross rent multipliers in the sales comparison approach, using data and capitalization rates from the income approach, is presented.

The various value approaches cannot be properly processed until the highest and best use of the property has been determined by preliminary analysis of available market data. A significant part of this conclusion is the analysis of the economic unit, particularly if there is excess land or building area. Avoidance or neglect of this fundamental concept is frequently the basis for divergent value opinions.

The discussion of the sales comparison approach addresses the meaning of *market comparability,* illustrates the use of paired transactions to de-

41

rive market adjustments, and examines the determination of units of comparison.

The income approach chapter begins with a discussion of the various methods for determining rentable area and the potential for variances. Vacancy allowances, as they relate to typical tenant-occupied and owner-occupied buildings, are discussed. Various types of expenses are discussed with particular emphasis on ad valorem taxes and the management expense charged to owner-occupied facilities. Replacement reserves are discussed in sufficient detail to indicate their probable effect on capitalization rate derivation. The chapter concludes with a discussion of various types of rates and the pitfalls of using improper methods for rate derivation.

The cost approach is frequently avoided by appraisers because it is extremely difficult to support cost-new estimates and to measure depreciation. Examples are presented to eliminate some confusion and illustrate the relationship of pertinent cost observations to other value approaches. Particular consideration is given to depreciation analyses and economic lives.

Section 2 concludes with a discussion of the reconciliation of the value indications produced by the various approaches and the bases for allocating value according to legal and financial interests or physical assets.

The Appraisal Process

Appraisers usually are aware of various processes, approaches, techniques, and methods that can be applied to the valuation of real property. It is a common misconception that the appraiser should, or must, use the ①sales comparison, ②income, and ③cost approaches in each appraisal for the value conclusion to have validity.

THE THREE APPROACHES

Appraisers frequently fail to relate the three valuation approaches when they use them. The three classic approaches are designed to reflect the respective comparative (sales comparison), economic (income), and physical (cost) characteristics of the subject property. Because each approach emphasizes one major attribute of the property, the level of confidence in the value conclusion is increased by using all applicable approaches, presuming that each is documented and reflects the proper use of logic. It is always better to avoid the use of a poorly supported approach than to blindly satisfy the mandate of using all three approaches.

The sales comparison approach stresses the comparative characteristics of reasonably competitive properties. This approach is appropriately used when there are sufficient market data to abstract units of comparison and support market adjustments for items of dissimilarity between the subject and comparable properties. The sales comparison approach is weakened if the "comparables" are not truly competitive on or about the appraisal date.

The income approach attempts to simulate the economics of a particular property and can be most useful if the appraisal subject has the potential for rental or sale as an investment property. The approach is weakened if there isn't enough data to support estimates of economic rent, operating expenses, and the selection of capitalization rates.

The cost approach stresses the physical characteristics of the improvements and the economic value of the land. This approach is most useful as a value indicator when the improvements are new or nearly new and reasonably reflect the optimum use of the site. Estimations of cost new and accrued depreciation affecting improvements that are in mid-life or older are usually considered by knowledgeable and professional appraisers to be futile efforts. This approach is generally used to estimate the value of special purpose real property where there may be little potential for sale or lease in the market.

The intricacies of the various valuation processes, analyses of certain problem areas, and the interrelationship of the three approaches will be discussed in the following sections.

It should be noted that each of these approaches produces an indication of market value, but the final market value estimate is concluded from the correlation or reconciliation of the valuation approaches utilized. In most appraisals, one or two of the approaches will be more applicable or more appropriate as subject value indicators. A wise appraiser will recognize the strengths and weaknesses of the market data and the relative reliability of the processes used in deriving the value conclusions.

RULES OF THUMB IN THE APPRAISAL PROCESS

Rules of thumb are frequently used as indicators of value or value ranges by real property investors, salespeople, lenders, and appraisers, but market support and the method of derivation directly affect their validity. Certain rules of thumb can be useful if the analyst exercises caution in their application, but the user should be fully aware of the accompanying hazards.

Some rules of thumb casually used in simple and complex appraisal problems include gross rent multipliers, capitalization rates, and expense ratios or percentages; all of these will be discussed in this section. The relationship between gross rent multipliers, capitalization rates, and net income estimates will be discussed to suggest a method for testing the validity of using these rules of thumb.

Gross Rent Multipliers

The gross rent multiplier is perhaps most frequently misused as an unsupported rule of thumb. It is simply the direct relationship between gross revenue and either price or value. A multiplier is usually calculated with gross annual rent for income properties and with monthly rents for single-family residential properties.

This variable does not consider operational efficiencies or deficiencies, or how actual rentals relate to market potential. Instead, the multiplier is computed by dividing one fact (price) by another (actual rents).

The multiplier will be significantly different if assumptions vary regarding the timing of rent collections and the inclusion or exclusion of utilities or furniture in the rental rate. Multipliers tend to be lower in management-intensive projects such as hotels or furnished apartment complexes operated on a daily or weekly rental basis.

Example A. A furnished apartment project with a scheduled weekly rental of $500 sold for $50,000. The gross rent multiplier is computed:

$$\frac{\text{Price}}{\text{Annual rent}} = \frac{\$50,000}{\$500 \times 52 \text{ weeks}} = \frac{\$50,000}{\$26,000} = 1.92$$

Example B. A warehouse with a scheduled monthly rental of $1,800 sold for $175,000. The gross rent multiplier is computed:

$$\frac{\$175,000}{\$1,800 \times 12 \text{ months}} = \frac{\$175,000}{\$21,600} = 8.10$$

Example C. A residence with a gross monthly rental of $450 sold for $50,000. The monthly rent multiplier is computed:

$$\frac{\text{Price}}{\text{Monthly rent}} = \frac{\$50,000}{\$450} = 111.11$$

Observation of these multipliers does not reveal any inherent assumptions or facts about management, collections, vacancy, or expense ratios. A prudent investor or analyst will be cautious about the derivation and application of the multiplier if this capitalization method is selected.

Capitalization Rates

A capitalization rate is defined as the rate that converts a periodic income amount into the cost or value of a capital asset. The amount of money in a savings account (value of asset) can be accurately determined if the periodic dividend (net income) and rate of discount (capitalization rate) for the corresponding discount period are known. A savings account earning $10,000 per annum, based on an interest rate of 5.5% per annum with annual compounding, has a capital asset value computed as follows:

$$\frac{\text{Income}}{\text{Rate}} = \frac{\$10,000}{.055} = \$181,818$$

If the interest were compounded daily, the capital asset value would be computed:

$$\frac{(\$10,000 \div 365)}{(.055 \div 365)} = \frac{\$27.40}{.00015} = \$182,667$$

Therefore, the more frequent the interest payment, the greater the value estimate.

There are many types of capitalization rates and caution must be exercised to ensure that: 1) the proper type of rate is used, and 2) the derivation of the rate used is consistent with the assumptions inherent in the subject property. Simply using a rule of thumb rate of 10% doesn't indicate whether the rate is an overall rate, a building rate, an interest, risk, or discount rate, an equity yield rate, a cash flow rate, or one of many other types of rates. It also doesn't indicate whether the rate reflects gross income or net income, including or excluding replacement reserves.

Minor variations in the capitalization rate can cause substantial differences in the value conclusions. For example:

$10,000 net income ÷ .10 (cap. rate) = $100,000 value
$10,000 net income ÷ .11 (cap. rate) = $ 90,910 value

Accordingly, extreme caution must be exercised in the capitalization process. Use of various residual techniques compounds the mathematical problems because different rates are applied to land and building components.

Expense Ratios and Percentages

The ongoing costs of an investment are generally classified as expenses, and are further identified as "fixed" expenses, such as ad valorem taxes and insurance, and "operating" expenses. Expenses usually are estimated to derive an estimate of annual net operating income, which can be converted into a value indication by capitalization.

Expense estimates, expressed as a percentage of income, will depend on one or more factors such as: 1) quality of construction, which affects the costs of maintenance and the consumption of utilities; 2) whether utilities are separately metered or expenses are otherwise passed on to tenants; 3) whether rents are at market levels, excessive, or depressed; 4) what types of concessions are made to tenants; and 5) the quality of management, including its ability to establish and collect proper rents, control vacancy and collection losses, and employ and supervise sufficient personnel. Each of these factors is significant; another category, known as "replacement reserves," also directly affects net income as a percentage of gross rent. Because all of these factors are variable, extreme caution should be exercised in casually utilizing rules of thumb regarding expenses and net income.

Testing the Capitalization Rate with the Rent Multiplier

The gross rent multiplier used by the appraiser, or implied by the appraisal, can be tested for its appropriateness and consistency by comparing it with the overall capitalization rate used in the income approach, or implied by the appraisal.

A multiplier is usually a "gross" rental factor which can be converted into a "gross" capitalization rate by taking its reciprocal (dividing into 1.0). If either the percentage of operating expense or the net income is known, the gross multiplier can be converted into an indicated overall capitalization rate.

The overall rate (R) is derived using the following formula, where: $I =$ net income as a percentage of gross income and V, or value, $=$ gross rent multiplier. A property with a 60% net income estimate selling for a rent multiplier of 7.0 reflects an overall rate computed as follows:

$$\frac{I}{V} = R, \quad \text{or} \quad \frac{.60}{7.0} = .08571, \text{ or } 8.571\%$$

Assume that the appraiser used a 9.25% overall rate to capitalize the net income into a value indication which, when divided by the gross annual rent, reflects a 7.0 gross rent multiplier. Further assume that the net income estimate represents 60% of the gross rent potential at full occupancy. Both sides of the preceding equation $(I/V = R)$ must equate if the appraiser has used the valuation approaches consistently.

There is an inconsistency in the two developed rates, so the appraiser must have misjudged in estimating: 1) the net income percentage, 2) the overall rate, or 3) the rent multiplier. This method can be useful in testing the validity of the income property appraiser's assumptions and value conclusions.

ECONOMIC UNIT DETERMINATION

The various valuation approaches cannot be properly processed until the economic unit has been defined, particularly where excess land is involved. An economic unit is essentially a site or a building which has the proper size, configuration, and functionality to provide the optimum return on the real estate. Failure to recognize the proper economic unit sets the stage for improper value conclusions and divergent value opinions.

The term "economic unit" commonly relates to the land area that is necessary to satisfy either: 1) the improvements for an existing use, or 2) the improvements which will likely be constructed on the site, if developed to its optimum use. Accordingly, the economic unit will not include excess land.

Proper estimation of the economic land unit is essential because the economic viability of the facilities could be affected. If the site is either inadequate or superadequate, the real estate entity will not be capable of producing an optimum return and will cause funtional obsolescence of the improvements.

The most profitable use includes a proper balance of all economic units in production, specifically labor, coordination, capital, and land. Excess land will minimize the overall value as net rents will be allocated over the larger land area, resulting in a lower unit value. Inadequate land areas will cause rent penalties, which will also lower unit values.

Determination of economic units for certain land uses is relatively simple and can be estimated by casual observation in some markets. This is particularly true when analyzing major service stations or fast-food restaurant sites where industry averages are reasonably well established. The appraiser should be careful to ensure that the selected economic unit complies with zoning ordinance requirements for land area and street frontage and allows for sufficient building setbacks from streets and boundaries.

When estimating the economic land unit for an existing improvement such as a restaurant located on a large parcel, the analyst should also consider building size, location on the parcel, and potential seating capacity. Market data might strongly suggest the economic unit for a typical restaurant location, but the existing subject building with substantially greater or smaller size or capacity would require an atypical site.

Following are several examples for selecting proper economic units.

Example 1. A multistory building with 100,000 sq. ft. of gross area is designed to accommodate 100 two-bedroom apartment units and judged to have an average value of $75,000 per unit, or $75 per sq. ft. Analyses of market data reveal that recent sales for larger two-bedroom units of 1,100 square feet indicate a current market value of $70 per sq. ft.; sales of three-bedroom units of 1,200 sq. ft. suggest a market value of $60 per sq. ft. If the market is expected to rapidly absorb either type of unit, the optimum choice would undoubtedly be the two-bedroom unit containing 1,000 sq. ft. because this produces the greatest present worth.

Example 2. A 100-acre tract near an interchange of major highways is zoned for commercial use, and the economics of the area strongly suggest that a regional mall is feasible. Because a mall will generate large volumes of traffic, it is quite likely that a prudent developer will anticipate developing or selling several "spin-off" commercial sites. There might also be sufficient land available for apartment or office development.

A detailed market study reveals that the market will support 700,000 sq. ft. of retail space; this configuration will require a 4:1 land-to-building ratio, or approximately 65 acres for the shopping center, leaving 35 acres for auxiliary uses. The tract has sufficient frontage to accommodate approximately 800 front feet of spin-off sites without detrimentally affecting the proposed shopping center.

Additional market research reveals that the typical retail or service establishment in this market area requires 150 feet of depth and 100–150 feet of frontage. Therefore, the economic unit for the center is approximately 65 acres and spin-off sites have economic unit sizes ranging from 15,000 to 22,500 sq. ft. The probable use of the balance of the tract (approximately 32 acres) would be estimated by similar analyses.

Example 3. A 30,000-sq. ft. warehouse facility is constructed on a 2.67-acre site in a popular office/warehouse district. The entire site is fenced, but the building occupant doesn't use all of it. The site may have excess land area, and a detailed analysis of this property and competitive facilities will test this hypothesis.

The following chart suggests a method for determining the proper economic land unit of an office/warehouse property:

Parcel	Building Area (Sq.Ft.)	Land Area (Sq.Ft.)	Land-to-Building Ratio	Land Coverage
Subject	29,596	90,000	3.04:1	33%
A	35,000	122,839	3.51:1	28
B	32,500	89,734	2.76:1	36
C	22,000	44,431	2.02:1	50
D	24,870	57,935	2.33:1	43
E	17,400	37,000	2.13:1	47

The ratios of land to building areas at the comparative facilities are generally lower than at the subject, suggesting that the subject facility may include excess land. The comparative data reflect ratios ranging from 2.02:1–3.51:1; it appears that a satisfactory subject ratio will be 2.5:1, or a building covering 40% of the lot area. Therefore, a reasonable estimate of required or economic land area is calculated:

29,596 sq. ft. × 2.5 = 74,000 sq. ft.

The balance of the subject site (approximately 16,000 sq. ft.) is excess land. This area may be large enough and have sufficient frontage and depth to be marketable as a separate building site in this market.

It is quite conceivable that, in certain markets, the calculated excess area will be negligible, particularly if the typical sites measure between two and three acres and sites of less than one acre are not permissible as building sites. In these instances and where the "excess" land is not accessible, the committed site will essentially constitute an economic unit and there will be no "excess" land value. As reverse plottage will likely exist, the average value per square foot of land area will be reduced in such instances.

The Sales Comparison Approach

The sales comparison approach is based on the economic principle that a prudent purchaser will not pay more for a property than the price an equally desirable substitute property would bring in the open market at that approximate point in time. Founded on this principle of substitution, the sales comparison approach depends on detailed analyses of recent sales, current listings, purchase options, and offers to purchase as indicators of market attitudes concerning the ability of similar properties to satisfy anticipated objectives.

Using the sales comparison approach, the appraiser simulates the price each "comparable" property would sell for on the date of the subject appraisal if it were identical to the subject property. This simulation normally requires detailed market analyses to discern variances between the properties and the magnitude of adjustments to be made for dissimilarities. The subject and specific comparable properties are then compared, with percentage or monetary adjustments made for these dissimilarities.

DETERMINATION OF MARKET COMPARABILITY

The validity of value indications produced by the sales comparison approach depends on the true comparability of the data. Some real estate practitioners, including many appraisers, casually use the term "comparable" to signify a property sale or lease, but frequently the transaction is not comparable. Data cannot be considered comparable unless they meet the various tests of comparability. Basically, properties must be similar in physical, functional, and economic aspects because comparability is measured in terms of productive capacity, efficiency, and functionality. However, there are other factors that affect the ultimate determination of comparability.

In analyzing each item of market data, the appraiser must be aware of several factors, including: 1) motivations of buyers and sellers, 2) terms and conditions of sale, and 3) competitiveness. The sale must reflect all the factors inherent in the definition of market value to be used as a comparable by the appraiser.

The sale of an identical building on a lot of equal size with identical frontage, zoning, utilities, exposure, and even the same rent roll, management, and expense history might not be comparable with the subject property, although they are on contiguous sites. The two properties are physically, functionally, and economically identical—and this is rare indeed—but the sale may have been consummated under conditions or circumstances not considered representative of the presumed prudent buyer and seller. One or more of the parties to the transaction might have been motivated by factors that prompted a specific market action.

For example, an investor might be motivated to pay more than market value for a property because of his or her high tax bracket and the investment's effect on spendable income. Another investor might have to liquidate certain holdings for reasons that might not be revealed publicly.

Presuming the transaction is reasonably comparable in motivation, terms, and conditions of sale, the property must be rated as to its competitiveness. This factor relates to the ability of the property to satisfy the essential needs of the investor. If the buyer of the sale property would not have seriously considered the subject property, then the appraiser cannot consider the transaction truly comparable.

The preceding discussion should not be construed to suggest that noncomparable data should be ignored; certain noncomparable property data can be meaningful in the valuation process. Capitalization rates, multipliers, ratios, price measures, and other variables derived from this data can be useful in the comparative processes, although numerous differences may exist in the physical, functional, or economic attributes of the properties.

Controversy often develops when the appraiser uses market data from other neighborhoods, cities, or states. This is certainly understandable if adequate market data for the specific property type and market in the immediate subject area are available. A small medical office designed for owner occupancy probably would not be competitive, and therefore not comparable, with a similar property in another city or state unless the appraiser has determined that the economics of the cities are comparable.

On the other hand, appraisers of major property types such as convention hotels, hospitals, offices, regional shopping centers, and recreational facilities might find no historic evidence of sales of similar properties in the general area. These property types probably have investment appeal in regional, national, or international markets. Investors would likely consider geographically remote alternative investments to be competitive as evidenced by the huge portfolios held by major institutional investors throughout the nation and in other parts of the world. Comparative analyses of these widely scattered properties may be not only proper, but mandatory, in many instances, if market value is to be accurately estimated.

The ultimate test of comparability is an affirmative answer to the question: "Is the sale property sufficiently competitive as an investment to be considered a reasonable substitute for the subject property?" The effect of minor differences between the subject and sales properties can be appropriately expressed as market adjustments. The appraiser considers how "comparable" properties differ from the subject property; as properties typically differ in many respects, comparative analyses of paired sales are usually required to isolate the value of noted differences.

PAIRED SALES ANALYSIS

Analysis of paired sales, where one distinguishing variant is evident, reveals the market reaction to this dissimilarity. If this process is continued with further pairing of sales, the value of each of the variants can be market supported. Then, each "comparable" sale property can be compared with the subject property and adjustments made for noted dissimilarities to indicate the subject value.

The following examples illustrate market deduction of the value of variances between "paired" transactions.

Example 1. Two sales of vacant lots are comparable except for the 19-month period separating their dates of transfer. One property sold for $.16 per sq. ft. and the other sold 19 months later for $.20 per sq. ft. The difference of $.04 per sq. ft. represents 25% of the unit price of the base transaction; this variance is approximately 16% per year for the 1.58 year period.

Some may elect to use a 13% adjustment from analysis of the paired sales ($.04 ÷ $.20 = .20 ÷ 1.58 years = 13% per year), but this is erroneous because the enhancement should relate to the beginning base.

Example 2. Two vacant lots of similar size were sold at approximately the same time but they differ in their zoning classifications, although both have similar potential for development. One lot sold for $2.00 per sq. ft.

and the other for $2.20 per sq. ft. The $.20 difference equals 10%, which apparently reflects the second property's greater flexibility of use.

Example 3. Two residential sales are very similar except that Sale A is in less desirable condition and has approximately 137 more square feet of living area. Other paired sales analysis reveals that a $1,300 adjustment is reasonable for the difference in the condition of these dwellings. The depreciated improvement value of Sale A is $8,500. When this amount is adjusted downward $1,300 for condition, the value equals $7,200, which is $950 more than the depreciated improvement value of Sale B. That $950, divided by 137 square feet, indicates an adjustment of $6.93 per sq. ft. for the building area variance.

These values of noted variances could be used to assist the appraiser in isolating the value of other variances in the same market.

SELECTION OF APPROPRIATE UNITS OF COMPARISON

To use the various valuation methods in the sales comparison approach, market data must be reduced to usable and relevant units of comparison. It is of utmost importance that the units of comparison with the greatest correlation be established before they are applied to the subject valuation. The significance of this analysis will be demonstrated in the following discussion.

SITE VALUATION

A small, single-family residential lot, a one-acre service station site, a 10-acre apartment site, a 50-acre shopping center site, a 500-acre farm, and a 5- to 50-acre warehouse or industrial site may each be properly identified as a "site" for valuation purposes. A site, in essence, is an economic unit, a land area with sufficient frontage, depth, and shape-utility to satisfy the market for that specific land use in that location.

In the case of residential lots, the market data may be broken down into units of comparison yielding indications of price per proposed or permissible apartment unit, price per square foot of land area, price per square foot of usable land area, price per front foot, price per acre, or price per lot. One or more of these units of comparison will usually yield a pattern that will have particular applicability to the immediate valuation problem.

Several recent transactions involving similar apartment-zoned tracts reveal sales prices ranging $10,000–$20,000 per acre, but these numbers are relatively insignificant to the appraiser. These data are further analyzed to reflect sales prices ranging $1,200–$1,500 per permissible apartment unit.

Therefore, the appraiser has narrowed the range from 50% (or 100%) in the acreage price to approximately 20% (or 25%) in the unit price analysis. Adjustments to the unit prices for items of dissimilarity, when compared with the subject site, will suggest more reasonable subject value indicators.

Residential lots in subdivisions usually áre consistent in terms of frontage and area, but when prices are analyzed by square foot or front foot, they might not offer a pattern as discrete as price per lot. Excess land area and frontage usually do not command as great a price premium as the land area or frontage of the basic economic unit. If residential lots of 35,000–40,000 sq. ft. typically sell for $9,500–$10,000 each, a 50,000-sq. ft. lot in the subdivision will not likely sell for $12,500, or a 25% premium, although the site is 25% larger and might include greater frontage.

Commercial, industrial, and some residential parcels may be analyzed on the bases of price per square foot and price per front foot. Caution must be exercised regarding extreme variances in depth and proper relationships of frontage to depth and frontage to land area. This is reflected by the data in the following table.

Parcel	Area (Sq. Ft.)	Frontage	Depth	Price Total	Per Sq. Ft.	Per Fr. Ft.
A	15,000	100´	150´	$15,000	$1.00	$150
B	20,000	100´	200´	17,000	.85	170
C	10,000	100´	100´	13,000	1.30	130
D	5,000	100´	50´	10,000	2.00	100

Assuming that Parcel A is the typical economic site containing 15,000 sq. ft. with 100 feet of frontage and 150 feet of depth, sites with much greater depths will usually sell for a greater price per front foot but a lower price per square foot. Sites with less depth will conversely sell for a lower price per front foot but a higher price per square foot.

Appraisers and investors frequently err by valuing typical lots using a front foot unit of comparison when the data reflect lots with extremely deep or shallow depths. In the preceding example, Parcel A, which represents the typical lot, is smaller and has less depth than Parcel B, which sold for about 15% more per square foot and about 13% more per front foot. However, Parcel A has less area but more depth than Parcel C, which sold for about 30% more per square foot and about 13% less per front foot.

VALUATION OF IMPROVED PROPERTY

Total transaction prices can be analyzed on the bases of price per square foot of gross building area, price per square foot of usable area, price per square foot of net rentable area, price per unit, price per room, or some other common unit of comparison.

Some units of comparison are more applicable to the specific appraisal problem than others and selecting the wrong unit of comparison will result in a distorted value conclusion. For example, it would be incorrect to use price per apartment unit when appraising a complex with one-bedroom units of 700 sq. ft. each when the market data reflect complexes with larger two- and three-bedroom units and smaller efficiency units. This is demonstrated in the following chart.

Project	Unit Type	No. of Units	Rooms	Gross Area (Sq. Ft.)	Price Per Unit	Per Room	Per Sq. Ft.
Subject	1 br	100	300	70,000			
1	1 & 2 brs	95	320	75,000	$13,000	$3,860	$16.47
2	2 brs	84	336	77,500	15,000	3,750	16.26
3	2 & 3 brs	126	567	127,500	17,000	3,778	16.80
4	3 brs	70	350	77,000	20,000	4,000	18.18

These data reflect prices ranging $13,000–$20,000 per unit, but the sales prices per room and per square foot of apartment area fall within relatively narrow ranges. The appraiser's correlation of these data, using these two units of comparison, should result in a meaningful value conclusion. Use of the price per unit would be meaningless unless the data were further analyzed for unit mix and price allocations were made before this unit of comparison was applied to the subject valuation.

In valuing functional buildings with market data on buildings which include substantial functional obsolescence, it is advisable to analyze the data on the basis of price per usable square foot or price per net rentable square foot. In instances where the subject and comparable buildings have similar functionality, use of any unit of comparison will probably be appropriate, although one or more units of comparison might reflect a narrower range of value.

Most improved property transactions can be analyzed on the basis of price per square foot of building area, particularly where the improvements represent a major portion of the value of the property. In instances where land value represents a major part of the total consideration, it is quite acceptable to allocate the total price separately to land and improvements, and analyze the implied improvement price with appropriate units of comparison. When applying these data in the subject valuation, the estimate of improvement value will be added to the subject land value to derive an indication of the subject property value.

The Income Approach

The rationale of the income approach is the economic principle of anticipation, which suggests that the value of a property capable of producing real estate income is the present worth of anticipated future net benefits. The procedure begins by estimating potential gross revenue and deducting estimated fixed and operating expenses, income loss allowances, and replacement reserves, to reflect the estimated net annual income expectancy. The net income is converted into a value indication by capitalization.

The primary objective of most income analyses is to simulate the economic aspects of real property in order to convert the estimated net income into value by capitalization. Some income streams can be capitalized into perpetuity; for others, such as leased properties, the respective interests should be valued to correspond with the unexpired lease term. In all cases, the real property analyst must carefully address all factors affecting revenue, expenses, and investment risks.

The validity of the income approach as a value indicator depends on accurate estimates of economic or market rent, vacancy and collection loss, and fixed and operating expenses, and on thorough data analyses for selection and utilization of appropriate capitalization methods, techniques, and rates.

DETERMINATION OF RENTABLE AREA

Value estimates are frequently questionable because the appraiser, management, or owners are inconsistent in calculating rentable areas, particularly in office properties. Rentable areas may logically be calculated by different methods within the same building, particularly in multistory buildings with whole-floor and multi-tenant floor occupancy.

A dilemma frequently faced by the appraiser of single-tenant office property is the availability of only multi-tenant rental data, or vice versa. The rentable area of multi-tenant space is typically the gross area calculated as the product of: 1) the distance between the center of parallel party walls, and 2) the distance between the glassed surface of outside walls and the inside wall of common corridors. There is a trend in many market areas to also include a pro rata amount of common area, such as corridors, mechanical rooms, stairwells, elevator shafts, and lounge areas, as rentable area for each tenant of multi-tenant floors.

The rentable areas of single-tenant space, even within multistory buildings, typically include all areas within the exterior walls, calculated from the glass line. Whole-floor rentable areas in multi-tenant buildings typically exclude areas, such as stairwells and elevator shafts, which also serve other floors, but some tenant areas are calculated to include these areas. It is usually apparent that building efficiencies—the ratio of rentable area to gross building area—will vary with the method of area calculation.

The appraiser/analyst should be aware of this distinction. Using raw primary data from a manager or owner or simply reviewing the lease can mislead one into comparing rental rates and operating expense data of dissimilar areas.

Two buildings of identical construction and gross area (say, 10,000 sq. ft.) may have efficiencies of 100% for whole-floor occupancy (single tenancy) and 85% for multi-tenant occupancy. The buildings may have the same market rent potential, but the corresponding rental rates will differ because of the difference in rentable area. If the whole-floor rate is $8.50 per sq. ft., the multi-tenant rate will be $10.00 ($8.50 ÷ .85 = $10.00).

This procedure may be tested as follows:

Whole-floor rentable area	10,000 sq. ft.
Rental rate	× $8.50
Annual rent	$85,000
Multi-tenant area (10,000 × .85)	8,500 sq. ft.
Multi-tenant rental rate ($85,000 ÷ 8,500)	$10.00/sq. ft.

Presume whole-floor efficiency is 95% and multi-tenant efficiency is 85%; if the whole-floor rental rate is $9.00, then the multi-tenant rate equivalency would be $10.06 per sq. ft. It is first necessary to calculate the "efficiency differential" (.95 ÷ .85 = 1.1176). This differential, when multiplied by the whole-floor rate of $9.00, equals $10.06.

This rate may be tested as follows:

Whole-floor rentable area (10,000 sq. ft. × .95)	9,500 sq. ft.
Rental rate	× $9.00
Annual rent	$85,500
Multi-tenant area (10,000 × .85)	8,500 sq. ft.
Multi-tenant rental rate ($85,500 ÷ 8,500)	$10.06/sq. ft.

With this procedure, the appraiser can properly convert dissimilar rates into reliable rental value estimates.

DERIVATION OF GROSS INCOME ESTIMATE

With many types of income-producing investment properties, the present rent roll or lease digest may well indicate probable revenue, but prudent management will likely increase rents at the earliest opportunity. Accordingly, rent rolls at apartment projects typically reflect a wide range of rates because of escalating rents and varying lease expiration dates. Of course, rents sometimes decline in overbuilt and extremely competitive markets.

The appraiser begins the analysis by estimating potential annual revenue, based on economic conditions existing on the appraisal date. This estimate necessitates detailed analyses of current rent rolls and rents at competitive facilities. The appraiser must be aware that current rents may differ substantially from the current or historical collection experience of the property. The effective gross revenue, or annual collections, can be directly related to the quality of management and degree of collection effort.

The income property appraiser makes many decisions that affect successive stages of the income appraisal process; some of these decisions may be arbitrary and form the bases for disagreement. Appraisers may differ in their treatment of pet and security deposits, earned interest, forfeited deposits and delinquent rent charges, and revenue from services and concessions such as laundry and vending machines. In projecting stabilized revenue collections, the appraiser may elect to estimate revenue in terms of the current purchasing power of money, inflated dollars, or deflated dollars. It is most important that the capitalization rate derived from market analysis be developed in a manner consistent with the subject income and expense assumptions as to purchasing power.

Ancillary revenue from interest, concessions, forfeitures, and delinquent fees accruing to the project can be properly included in the appraisal process if reflected in the sale properties from which pertinent capitalization rates are derived.

In appraising business-oriented real property such as nursing homes, hospitals, hotels, and recreational/resort properties, it is of utmost importance that the appraiser either deduct sufficient entrepreneurial/ business profits or adjust the capitalization rate to reflect only the real property value. Otherwise, the appraisal will reflect the value of the total entity, both real property and business.

The estimate of market rent should be based on the lease or rental terms and on conditions prevailing in the specific market. If competitive properties are typically rented with the lessor responsible for payment of ad valorem taxes, property insurance, and costs for maintaining the roof and building exterior, the subject rent should be estimated accordingly unless adjustments are properly developed, supported, and discussed.

The appraiser must take care to determine the lease terms, responsibility of respective parties, date of contract, and whether the pertinent data relate to renewal options prescribed by an older lease. If these factors are ignored, the appraiser's estimate of current market rent could be influenced by irrelevant market data from otherwise comparable or competitive properties.

VACANCY ALLOWANCES

When estimating net operating income in the income approach, appraisers typically deduct from gross income potential an allowance for vacancy and/or collection losses. It is often argued that no charge should be made for this item in instances where a facility has been fully occupied for several years and the occupants are not likely to vacate the premises. This is erroneous, however, because in estimating market value, the appraiser begins with an estimate of market or economic rent, but it is quite likely that a long-term tenant or lessee is paying less than market rent. A vacancy or collection loss allowance would not be justified if contract rent is used for projection purposes. Such a process is a deviation from market value estimation and would include appraising a leased fee ownership interest.

The property may well experience no vacancy or collection losses because contract rent is less than market rent. If market rent is properly estimated, it is very likely that most properties will experience some vacancy or collection loss during the remaining economic or useful life of the improvements or the projected ownership period. Seldom are spaces occupied by new tenants on the same day a vacancy occurs, thus enabling full or continual occupancy. With office, warehouse, apartment, and retail properties in particular, it is likely that competent management will be unable to collect all contract rents because of financial difficulties or other circumstances affecting noncredit tenants.

Appraisers are often criticized for projecting a standard vacancy allowance of 5% per year; in actuality, there are no standards because this allowance should be a market phenomenon. The income loss allowance is partially dependent on the level of confidence the appraiser has in the estimate of market rent. The allowance will likely be affected by many other economic factors, including:

1. The ability of tenants to pay present market rents in the future. This might be influenced by announcements or anticipated announcements regarding employment cutbacks, plant closings, or expansions; union contracts; the purchasing power of money; utility rate increases; etc.
2. The appraiser's awareness of an impending oversupply of competitive space in the reasonable future.
3. Governmental or private restrictions that preclude new construction, although a strong, continuing demand appears to exist.

These factors, when properly analyzed, should influence the appraiser's estimate of the proper allowance to be made for vacancy and collection losses in the market rent estimate. It is quite logical to project an increased collection loss allowance for an office or apartment project in a market that reflects near 100% occupancy, when the appraiser/analyst anticipates that substantial new competitive space will enter and possibly saturate the market. Conversely, restrictions against new construction in a strong market might call for lower income losses, higher economic rents, or both.

Other vacancy-related problems which are common, but are not discussed in detail here, include:

1. The effect on market value of an extremely high vacancy rate as in the case of a new building expected to require several months or years to lease to a reasonable or stabilized occupancy level.
2. The effect on market value of multi-tenant facilities in which rental rates vary from substantially below to perhaps somewhat above present market levels and the rate of occupancy is low.

Should the appraiser deduct an allowance for vacancy and collection loss when appraising the owner-occupied facility? If the purpose of the appraisal is to estimate market value, no consideration will be given to the use, investment criteria, management, maintenance levels, or other facets peculiar to current ownership. If these factors enter into the valuation formula, the value conclusion will be either "investment value" or "value in use."

Any appraisal of market value should reflect market expectations. The appraiser estimates market rent and an income loss allowance assuming the property is available for rent on the open market on the date of appraisal.

Market rent is the gross income potential in current dollars on the appraisal date and this estimate must include any market-recognized prospects for income loss. This is considered realistic and practical when analyzing either tenant- or owner-occupied facilities.

ANALYSIS OF EXPENSES

The operating statements for a two- to three-year period are of primary concern to the prudent investor and to the appraiser because they provide financial operation summaries which improve the validity of projections. A single annual statement may be misleading as it may reflect major, nonrecurring expenditures.

The typical accountant's statement is designed for tax-reporting purposes and frequently includes expenditures and charges which relate to the ownership entity, including corporate franchise fees, salaries of executives, capital expenditures, tax depreciation, and mortgage interest. Corporate charges will not normally be considered legitimate real estate expenses unless the property will likely be sold and maintained as a part of a corporation. Executive salaries may legally be reflected as a corporate expense, but should not be considered a property expense if management expense is accounted for elsewhere.

The operating statement of a facility that is a part of a chain or larger enterprise may be misleading in several ways. It is not uncommon for an accountant to allocate total general and administrative expenses, insurance, and other expenses to respective properties based on business volume or the size of the facility. The facility may well benefit from economies of scale which would not exist if the specific property were operated independently. If the valuation involves only the subject property, the analyst should recognize this element and adjust the pertinent expenses to reflect any probable increase due to the loss of economies of scale.

Expense estimates for the subject property should be based on analyses of each subject expense, tested in comparison with operating expenses at competitive facilities. Management and ad valorem taxes are significant items of expense which are discussed in the following sections.

MANAGEMENT EXPENSE

Should the appraiser deduct an allowance for management expense in projecting the net operating income of a property that is owner-occupied or managed by the owner?

In estimating market value, the appraiser simulates market expectations of net operating income, which will be converted into a value estimate in the open market as of the appraisal date. Accordingly, the appraiser projects a reasonable estimate of market-derived expenses, including management. Management must be deducted as an expense item unless the property is to sell with the seller continuing to provide management services, at no expense to the new owner. However, the definition of market value presumes a transaction between prudent parties, and a prudent and knowledgeable seller would not provide management services to a succeeding owner without reasonable compensation.

By not deducting a management expense, the implied value of an owner-managed property would be greater than that of a professionally managed property. Presuming that a prudent person would anticipate reasonable compensation for services rendered, the premium relates to the value of the business management, which is not part of the real property appraised.

Therefore, it is most reasonable to deduct a management expense when projecting net income for income properties. The expense allowance should be equivalent to the prevailing cost of obtaining competent and aggressive management which will strive to maintain the property at adequate levels to obtain market rents, minimize expenses, and maximize returns to the owner over a sustained period of time. Prudent ownership would be justified in paying a reasonable fee for successful management.

ESTIMATING AD VALOREM TAX EXPENSE

Ad valorem taxes are a major item of fixed annual expense which affects the value indication in the income approach. The appraiser should be sure that the actual and projected taxes on improved properties are reasonable and consistent with the taxes on similar and competitive properties in the area because each expense dollar reduces the subject value indication. One method for determining the reasonableness of the current tax expense is to analyze the tax data of the subject and other similar properties into categories for comparison.

Ad valorem tax expenses can be further reduced to a percentage of either estimated gross market rent or gross contract rent. In instances where the subject or tax comparables include excess land, the assessment and taxes can be allocated separately to the land and the improvements for more exact analysis and projection of tax expenses for the economic unit.

These charted data on actual office/warehouse facilities strongly suggest that the subject assessment and taxes are exorbitant and an appeal to the taxing authority to lower the assessment is recommended. In projecting this expense item, the appraiser must consider the probability of successfully obtaining a tax reduction.

Property	Gross Building Area (Sq.Ft.)	Tax Appraisal	Tax Assessment	Current Year Taxes	Assessment Per Sq.Ft.	Annual Taxes Per Sq.Ft.
Subject	29,596	$472,050	$188,820	$11,008	$6.38	$.37
A	24,870	167,250	66,900	3,900	2.69	.16
B	35,000	265,875	106,350	6,200	3.04	.18
C	32,500	235,675	94,270	5,496	2.90	.17
D	17,400	148,575	59,430	3,465	3.42	.20
E	11,300	83,250	33,300	1,941	2.95	.17

In instances where tax comparables are unavailable and the subject improvements are either: 1) proposed improvements and therefore not currently taxed, or 2) taxed excessively, the appraiser is faced with a major dilemma. In processing the income approach into an indication of market value, a deduction for tax expense must be made, but the expense cannot be determined until value is ascertained. With no tax comparables, the best alternative is to adjust the capitalization rate for the anticipated tax expense and apply this loaded rate to the estimated net income before deducting taxes.

The estimated tax adjustment to the capitalization rate can be computed by multiplying the current millage rate by the assessment factor used by the taxing authority. That figure is multiplied by the prevailing percentage of assessment relative to known prices paid for other taxable properties in the tax district.

Presuming that: 1) the taxing authority assesses at 50% of its estimate of value, 2) tax appraisals have typically represented 80% of prevailing sales prices, and 3) the current millage rate is $6.00 per $100 of assessment, the annual tax expense or tax load would be approximately 2.4% of probable value, computed:

$$.50 \times .80 \times \frac{6.00}{100} = \frac{2.40}{100} = .024$$

If the appropriate overall capitalization rate would have otherwise been 9.5%, the adjusted rate to be applied to this higher, unadjusted net income would be:

Unadjusted rate	.0925
Tax load	.0240
Adjusted overall rate	.1165

This procedure can be tested using the preceding example. Assume that gross rent potential is $40,000 per year and deductions for income loss allowance and all expenses except taxes total approximately $9,000 per year. The net income, unadjusted for taxes, is therefore $31,000 per year; the indicated subject value is capitalized:

$31,000 ÷ .1165 = $266,094   Rounded $266,000

If the overall rate load for taxes is 2.4%, then the annual taxes would be 2.4% of $266,000, or $6,384 per year. If the unadjusted net income of $31,000 is adjusted downward for tax expense, the net income of $24,616 per annum capitalized at 9.25% would confirm the indicated value of $266,000.

DERIVATION OF NET INCOME ESTIMATE

Several synonymous terms for *net annual income* are used by income property appraisers; some are discussed here for clarification. These terms include: *net income before depreciation, net income before recapture, net operating income,* and *net income.*

Each of these terms identifies a net annual income estimate for the property after deducting vacancy and collection loss allowances, fixed expenses, operating expenses, and replacement reserve allowances from the estimate of annual market rent. No deductions from income are made for future depreciation because this item is more appropriately reflected in the recapture portion of the capitalization rate.

Frequently, appraisers deduct annual debt service and add back the replacement reserves to derive a net income estimate; this, however, is more appropriately identified as *cash flow* or *equity dividend.* The defined net income is then converted into a subject value indication by capitalization.

CAPITALIZATION

There is much controversy and abundant literature on the various methods and techniques for income capitalization and the derivation of capitalization rates. These techniques are essentially the result of different assumptions and different methods of investment recapture.

Prudent investors commit funds in anticipation of ultimately recovering the investment and with the incentive of receiving a periodic payment or return on the investment throughout the investment period. Investment recovery is sometimes called *recapture* or *return of investment,* and the incentive payment is called *interest* or *return on investment.* Investment returns are typically expressed as annual rates.

The investor who deposits funds in a passbook savings account anticipates earning the contract rate of interest as the return on investment and is confident that the investment, plus interest can be fully recovered at will. The capitalization rate for such an investment is the contract interest rate, which may be called the *discount rate.*

The imputed value of a capital asset can be calculated by dividing the pertinent net income by the appropriate capitalization rate. Thus, the capital value of a savings account is easily estimated by dividing the periodic interest earned by the interest rate. If the account earns $54.17 per month and the contract interest rate is 6.5% per year (compounded monthly), the present value of the investment is: $54.17 ÷ .0054167 = $10,000.

An investment in land is similar to a savings account insofar as full recovery will occur when the asset is sold. Therefore, the typical investor will anticipate a yield or return on the investment during the holding period. The total net rent and sale proceeds, after full investment recovery is provided, will be interest or return on investment.

The investor in improved real estate is typically faced with the prospects of future depreciation of the capital value of the improvements. His objectives are no different from the objectives of the saver or land investor; each investor wants a return on and recovery of the investment. The improved property investor is usually less assured of full recovery upon lease expiration or sale of the assets and he therefore protects the investment by requiring a periodic return of the investment in the wasting assets. To attract prudent investors, the property's net operating income must be sufficient to provide for recapture and a satisfactory annual return on the investment price.

Capitalization Methods and Techniques

The appraiser of improved real estate must select the method and technique that best reflect the typical investor's attitude about recapture, based on market observations.

Direct capitalization is perhaps the simplest method as it directly applies an overall rate of return to the net income estimate to obtain a value indication. The overall rate is a blended rate providing for return on and of the capital investment.

Straight capitalization, like direct capitalization, does not utilize compound interest functions. The significant difference is that the land residual, building residual, and property residual techniques used in straight capitalization require allocation of net income to the interest and recapture portions of the investment.

The land and building residual techniques are designed to facilitate the valuation of the unknown part when either the land value (ascertained from market observation) or the building cost or value is known. The use of straight capitalization always implies that the net operating income is declining on a straight-line basis, reflecting a decreasing return on the declining investment.

Annuity capitalization uses compound interest functions and allocates net income to the interest and recapture portions of the investment. With annuity capitalization, net income estimates must be predictable and follow a schedule. It should be noted that annuities can be level, increasing, or decreasing and that building residual, land residual, and property residual techniques can be processed with annuity capitalization.

The valuation of lease interests and other partial or undivided interests invariably requires the use of compound interest functions.

The proper use of direct capitalization demands that the subject and sale properties from which the overall rate is developed be very similar in age and quality of improvements and exhibit the same relationship of land value to total value. If the land value ratios vary substantially, the net income estimates for the property with the higher land ratio would theoretically be lower as there would be less recapture. When the ratios are dissimilar, straight capitalization may be more appropriate unless the investment has the characteristics of an annuity; in that case, annuity capitalization would be more appropriate.

Many contemporary appraisers have essentially stopped using the residual techniques in favor of direct capitalization with rates derived by mortgage-equity analysis. The residual techniques are quite valid for use in appraising many structures, but straight capitalization with straight-line recapture is valid only when the buildings are very old and net income is expected to decline annually on a straight-line basis, or when the improvements are nearing the end of their economic life. In the latter case, a relatively new building could have a short remaining life if the land value represents most of the total property value and land appreciation is expected to continue.

Annuity capitalization utilizing the residual techniques is considered quite appropriate as a primary valuation method or to confirm the value indication by direct capitalization.

USE AND ABUSE OF REPLACEMENT RESERVES

The appraiser of income-producing real property typically deducts a periodic (usually annual) allowance as a reserve item in deriving an estimate of net operating income. The reserve might include allowances for replacing roof cover, floor covering, store front, heating and air conditioning equipment, lighting fixtures, asphalt paving, and other items.

Many investors, realty agents, and lenders argue that typical owners do not establish and maintain reserve accounts for replacement of short-lived components; they contend that the appraiser who projects a reserve is out of touch with reality. Appraisers will likely agree that a reserve account is not customary, but the concept is still valid.

In projecting the probable operating statement for the property being appraised, the appraiser typically analyzes historical expense statements for the subject and competitive facilities. These expense statements might reflect erratic expenditures for "reserve" items or none at all. From these statements, the appraiser must accurately anticipate the probable net annual income before debt service to produce a conclusion of market value that is accurate and supportable.

Effect of Replacement Reserves on Capitalization Rates

The net income estimate is converted into an indication of market value by using the appropriate capitalization method. For purposes of this discussion, a direct method with an overall capitalization rate is used.

To select the appropriate capitalization rate, the appraiser should analyze several market transactions for indications of investors' anticipated overall rates of return. In the analytic process, the appraiser's estimated annual operating expenses and reserves are typically deducted from the estimated annual income potential. The residual net operating income before debt service is then divided by the actual sale price to yield the indicated overall rate for the sale property. This process is repeated for all sales of similar and competitive properties available for analysis.

Presume that four sales of similar properties were analyzed in this manner and reflect the following data:

Sale	Annual Gross Income	Expenses and Reserves	Net Income	Sale Price	Overall Rate
1	$150,000	$ 57,750	$ 92,250	$ 900,000	10.25%
2	200,000	91,760	108,240	1,100,000	9.84
3	258,000	108,070	149,930	1,450,000	10.34
4	230,000	99,170	130,830	1,225,000	10.68

Further presume that the appraiser estimates a net operating income of $105,000 for the subject property, after deducting an annual allowance of

$2,500 for replacement reserves. He concludes from the market data analyzed that the appropriate overall capitalization rate for the subject property is 10.25%. The indicated subject value is computed at $1,024,390 ($105,000 ÷ .1025) and rounded to $1,025,000.

If the appraiser had elected not to deduct an allowance for replacement reserves, the net income estimates of the sale and subject properties would have been approximately $2,500 greater. With greater net income, each sale would have reflected a higher overall rate, as calculated below:

Sale	Adjusted Net Income	Sale Price	Overall Rate*
1	$ 94,750	$ 900,000	10.53%
2	110,740	1,100,000	10.07
3	152,430	1,450,000	10.51
4	133,330	1,225,000	10.88

*Excluding reserves

From analysis of these data, the appraiser would logically select a higher overall rate, perhaps 10.5%–10.75%, to reflect the higher estimate of subject net income when reserves are not considered. The adjusted subject net income of $107,500, divided by the 10.5% overall rate, reflects an indicated subject value of $1,023,810, which also may be rounded to $1,025,000.

The final market value indication will not be affected if the capitalization process is performed accurately. The determination of the use of replacement reserves must be consistent with the method of treating the sales data from which the capitalization rates are derived.

In reality, it does not matter which method is used. In theory, it is considered more accurate to deduct replacement reserves before capitalization because the various sale properties, as well as the subject, typically have variances in type and amount of furnishings, equipment, and age. These factors, and the timing of needed replacement, affect the amount of periodic replacement allowance.

Philosophies and Methods of Estimating Reserves

The theory behind replacement reserves is that the owner deposits the estimated allowance in a fund at the end of each year to assure accumulation of an amount sufficient to replace expired items when necessary. Philosophies regarding the estimation of replacement reserves differ among professional appraisers. Some appraisers insist that the estimated present cost of replacing a specific short-lived item should be divided by the number of years in its normal useful life, i.e., years between expected replacement periods (Premise A). Others insist that the estimated cost of replacement should be multiplied by the number of replacements that will be needed during the remaining economic or useful life of the improvements; then, this product is divided by the estimated years of remaining economic life to establish an annual reserve amount (Premise B).

Presuming that the current replacement cost of an item is approximately $1,000 and its normal useful life is 10 years, under Premise A, the straight-line reserve allowance would equal $100 per year. If the item is located in a new building which is judged to have a 50-year economic life, it will require replacement four times. Therefore, under Premise B, $4,000 ($1,000 × 4) divided by 50 years (remaining economic life of the building) equals $80 per year.

Premises A and B produce substantially different reserve requirements, yet both use the straight-line concept, which is also controversial.

Premise A requires the largest annual reserve deposit for the specific item during all but the last 10 years of the anticipated building life. There would be no reserve during the last period as the item would probably not be replaced.

Premise B is judged to be erroneous in concept because the required replacement dollars are allocated over each year of the anticipated building life. This is unrealistic as the item has already been installed and will presumably last 10 years. Reserves should be established during this 10-year period to provide a replacement item for the next 10-year period. Accordingly, in this example, the total required replacement dollars should be divided by only 40 years; thus, the straight-line reserve requirement will be consistent with the one produced with Premise A, i.e., $100 per year.

Replacement reserves are often erroneously established by relating the cost of replacement to the remaining useful life of the item, instead of the full-term useful life if new. The concept of replacement reserves requires a deposit each year, except during the final years of the building life after the last replacement.

If an item costing $1,000 has a five-year remaining useful life, this method will require an annual deposit of $200 for five years. Thereafter, the $1,000 replacement will be provided for by a reserve created by straight-line deposits of $100 per year. Because the appraiser typically estimates annualized expenses, this inconsistency must be avoided. This statement should not be construed as ignoring the probability of either deferred maintenance or value diminution; the physical status of this wasting asset will require full replacement in five years, although only half of the theoretical reserve will have been accumulated upon life expiration.

If the short-lived item would normally require replacement after 10 years of use and it is in its ninth year, but the overall building is judged to have a remaining useful or economic life of only five or six years, it is quite likely that a prudent owner would try to extend the life of the item by maintenance and not replace it. Accordingly, a reserve for replacement would be illogical in such instances.

Reserve Accumulation: Straight-Line vs. Sinking Fund

One controversial aspect of replacement reserves relates to how they are accumulated. The preceding discussion has included the assumption that periodic deposits will be made on a straight-line basis during the reserve period. If reserve accounts are theoretically advisable and utilized by appraisers, who simulate the actions of prudent owners and investors, it is only logical that a prudent owner would deposit funds in a sinking-fund, interest-bearing account, which contrasts sharply with the straight-line concept. The prudent owner would, theoretically, expect to make periodic deposits into the sinking fund account, which, with interest, would increase to an amount theoretically sufficient to replace the expired item when needed. A replacement reserve is not logical in theory or in practice if it assumes imprudent ownership.

As interest is earned on the sinking fund, this type of replacement reserve would require a lower annual deposit. Accordingly, the higher estimated annual net operating income would appear to capitalize into a higher capital value than would result from utilization of a straight-line reserve.

The appraiser can properly use either straight-line or sinking-fund methods of funding the theoretical replacement reserves, provided that consistency is maintained when analyzing sales data from which capitalization rates are derived. The capitalization rates will vary depending on the method of funding selected, but the capitalized value of the appraised property should not fluctuate.

If the investor elects not to fund the reserve account, a prospective purchaser would probably analyze the likelihood of replacing items during the anticipated ownership period and adjust the purchase price or offer accordingly. Regardless of the practices of investors in the marketplace, the concept of replacement reserves is judged to be most appropriate for value analysis.

DERIVATION AND APPLICATION OF
CAPITALIZATION RATES

Perhaps the most controversial aspects of income property valuation relate to selecting a capitalization method and technique and deriving a
proper rate or rates for application in the capitalization process. Every capitalization method and technique requires the use of at least one type of rate
to provide for interest and investment recapture.

Of the many types of rates available, some are applicable in the residual
techniques, but cannot be properly used when processing the value indication by direct capitalization. Other types of rates are applicable in the development method, but are not properly used elsewhere. It is imperative that
the appraiser thoroughly understand the characteristics, method of derivation, and rationale of all rates used in the valuation.

Although any rate used to convert income or future benefits into a capital value is essentially a capitalization rate, most real estate practitioners
prefer to adopt some particular type of rate for simplicity or practicality of
use. Accordingly, the topic of capitalization rates is usually quite controversial.

It is important to realize that gross income to the property can be allocated only to expenses (including reserves) or to the net income that is available to satisfy debt and equity requirements. Although debt service must be
satisfied first, this does not preclude net income before debt service from
further analysis on a "free and clear" basis.

Misunderstandings may arise among investors, lenders, real estate salespeople, appraisers, and others because of distinct differences in terminology, methods of income analysis, and objectives. Investors and the broker-
age sector typically consider cash flow the most significant aspect of the
investment, but they may also consider the gross rent multiplier, which is a
type of direct capitalization method. Lenders are usually most concerned
about debt-coverage ratios and the property's ability to produce positive
cash flows. They typically want to determine the overall rate of return,
the prospective equity yield rate, and the cash flow rate to the equity investors; these factors influence the underwriting of the risks of mortgagor
default.

Various types of capitalization rates used in real estate and related industries are discussed below.

1. *Discount rate.* The most elemental capitalization rate is the discount
   rate, which is frequently called the *property interest rate* or *risk rate.*
   This rate is essentially the annualized net return on the total current
   capital investment in land and improvements. The derived rate of return is based on current net income (actual or estimated) before debt-

service payments; therefore, the effects of leverage are excluded. The rate is basic and does not reflect the recapture or return "of" any part of the investment, which might be classified as depreciation. The discount rate is the purest of all rates because it is truly an unadjusted rate of return which does not consider the investment's effects on the specific investor. The discount rate is particularly useful in processing the residual techniques and in valuing lease interests and other annuities. Discount rates are reliably derived by analyzing sales of competitive properties. The total annual net income of the sale property is allocated to provide recapture, or the periodic return of the improvements, and the balance is imputed to the return on the land and improvements. This latter income is related to the total price to reflect the interest or discount rate.

2. *Recapture rate.* This is the annual provision for the future depreciation of improvements. The prudent investor would anticipate an annual net income sufficient to provide for recapture of any value decline.

3. *Building capitalization rate.* This rate is comprised of the sum of the discount or interest rate and the recapture rate. It is used with the residual techniques.

4. *Overall rate.* This rate is simply net operating income divided by the sale price or value. The rate is typically derived after deducting all expenses and replacement reserves from the "effective gross income" for the fee simple property. Accordingly, the overall rate will be different if reserves are not deducted or if contract rent is used instead of market rent. If contract rent differs from market rent, the use of contract rent will reflect an overall rate for the leased fee interest. The overall rate is a blended rate which provides for *all* interests in the property, including: 1) property interest/discount, 2) building recapture, 3) mortgage interest, 4) amortization, 5) cash flow or equity dividend, and 6) property yield or internal rate. The overall rate will also reflect any leasehold or leased fee rates, if applicable. The overall rate can be further analyzed to reflect the effects of the mortgage and equity components.

5. *Equity dividend, cash flow, or cash-on-cash rate.* These are synonymous terms for the annual rate of cash flow on the original equity. This is calculated by dividing net annual income (including replacement reserves) after debt service by the original equity investment.

6. *Yield rate.* Yield, frequently confused with cash flow, is a term that includes the annualized composite effects of: 1) cash flow, 2) the buildup of equity through debt amortization, and 3) any overall

value appreciation or decline during the ownership or projection period. The yield rate is an annualized rate relating to the equity investment, and is essentially synonymous with the internal rate of return. The internal rate is typically used to reflect historical before- or after-tax yields.

The principal difference among the various capitalization techniques and methods lies in their assumptions concerning capital recovery and the reinvestment of recovered funds. Capital recovery may be provided on the basis of straight-line, sinking-fund, or annuity concepts. Straight-line recapture presumes that recovered assets will not be reinvested; the sinking-fund method of recapture presumes reinvestment of assets at the "safe" rate, which may be the prevailing passbook interest rate offered by savings and loan associations. For properties having the characteristics of an annuity, recaptured funds are presumed to be reinvested at the property risk/interest rate. Use of the overall rate as an analytic tool implies that recaptured proceeds are reinvested in the same, or at least a similar, property at the equity yield rate. This is the basis for concluding that the equity yield and internal rates are synonymous.

Many contemporary appraisers consider the use of mortgage-equity analyses to be the only meaningful way to develop a capitalization rate. This thinking is fallacious as it generally presumes that all properties have a constant net income until the day when income abruptly stops and the buildings have no economic value. Although mortgage-equity techniques are excellent tools for analyzing market transactions, they cannot develop rates merely by referring to prevailing mortgage rates and terms and presumed equity requirements. This process develops "nonmarket" rates, and the value judgment can hardly be called "market value" if the overall rates are not market-derived.

The mortgage-equity method can be properly used to analyze overall market rates into two components: mortgage and equity, which includes cash flow, anticipated value change, and yield. With sufficient market data properly analyzed, the appraiser should be able to use the mortgage-equity techniques to synthesize supportable "market-derived" overall capitalization rates.

In addition to the complex problem of deriving market capitalization rates, the appraiser frequently must estimate or select a discount rate for specific application. In many instances, these rates are not market supportable and it is necessary to rely on logical analyses of general and nonmarket data. The following situations illustrate this problem.

Example 1. Presume that there is no market support for a rate that will discount net income or cash losses during the stabilization of operations at recently constructed or existing, but troubled, projects. How can the analyst determine or select the proper type of rate to discount the anticipated losses?

The overall rate abstracted from the market would not be the proper rate because it includes all the ingredients of the investment, of which cash flow is only a part. The overall rate also includes provision for capital recovery or recapture and reflects any anticipated value change plus the effects of any mortgage amortization.

The use of a nonrealty-based discount rate, such as a bond yield rate, also would be improper because it does not account for the realty investment's tax advantages, including the lower capital gains tax treatment.

Example 2. In the estimation of a fair return, such as the value of a temporary easement, market determination of the proper discount rate may be questionable if the overall rate is the primary basis of analysis. The easement is temporary and therefore differs substantially from the characteristics of the entire property, which are represented by the overall rate. The overall rate reflects any anticipated value change, mortgage amortization, and cash flow. Also, the overall rate reflects a net return, while the easement demands a gross return because the subservient estate is responsible for ad valorem taxes.

One area of particular concern is the stratification of rates for various property interests and components represented in the real estate. The real property in its entirety may be represented by an overall capitalization rate, which provides for return on investment plus capital recovery. Because the overall rate represents the total property, it includes the stratification of all physical, legal, and financial interests. The legal and financial interests are of particular concern here, specifically leased fee and leasehold rates and the mortgage and equity rates on financed property.

For any investment property, a positive leasehold is more exposed to the risks of loss than a leased fee interest. Real equity is more vulnerable than the mortgaged portion of the investment. Accordingly, the appraiser should consider the comparative attributes of leasehold versus equity and leased fee versus mortgage in selecting the proper capitalization/discount rate for the particular valuation. This observation is particularly significant where leasehold market data are limited and alternative analyses and consideration of equity rates of return are necessary.

A frequent error among appraisers is using rates developed by analysis of leased properties for fee simple valuation problems. A leased fee rate reflects a safer position than fee simple and a lower rate. Therefore, applying this rate to a net income representing fee simple would produce an inflated value estimate. Applying an overall rate derived from fee simple transactions to a leased fee income would also produce an erroneous value estimate.

The appraiser is an interpreter of the market and should be reasonably familiar with the types of rates used by the various segments of the market. The qualified appraiser/analyst can convert rates for further analysis and use them in valuation or investment counseling.

Appraisers frequently are asked to cite the capitalization rate or gross rent multiplier currently used in appraising a particular property type. Such requests are usually made by people who are aware that there is no established marketplace for real property like the one for marketing securities. There are no absolute rates that the appraiser can use in all appraisals of similar properties, just as all stocks do not sell at the same price-earnings ratio.

The selection of a capitalization rate is influenced by the appraiser's confidence in the analyses of rent and expenses, the remaining useful life estimated for the improvements, an analysis of the proper relationship of the contributory value of land and improvements to the total package, available or existing financing terms, costs of borrowing funds, and consideration of replacement reserves as an expense item. For business-oriented real estate such as hotels and proprietary hospitals, the rate will be significantly influenced by the treatment of business profits in the capitalization process.

The appraiser's ultimate decision must be influenced by detailed analysis of actual market transactions into comparable units for application in the subject valuation. The capitalization rate selected should be tailored to the capitalization method and technique that is consistent with the conditions or assumptions inherent in the property under appraisal.

The Cost Approach

The cost approach begins with an estimate of land value, usually assumed to be vacant and available for development to its optimum use. *Reproduction cost new* or *replacement cost new* is then estimated and followed by estimates of observed depreciation and obsolescence. The depreciated cost estimate is then added to the land value to yield a subject value indication.

The most vulnerable areas of the cost approach are the methods and concepts used to estimate cost new, determine the type and estimate the amount of depreciation/obsolescence, and differentiate between the useful and economic lives of improvements.

ESTIMATING COST NEW

The appraiser must make a major decision regarding the appropriate type of cost new to estimate. *Reproduction cost* is the estimated cost of reproducing facsimile improvements; *replacement cost* is the estimated cost of replacing them with improvements of equivalent utility as of a specific date. It is of utmost importance that improvement costs be estimated in terms of current dollars on the appraisal date, without concern for the improvements' actual cost if constructed many years earlier. This should not be construed to suggest that historical cost data cannot be factored for current usage.

The appraiser should consider the degree of functional obsolescence in the improvements and the availability of similar materials and workmanship in determining the type of cost new to estimate. It usually is considered impractical to estimate the reproduction cost new of an old or func-

77

tionally obsolete structure. Estimation of replacement cost new will theoretically provide like utility and eliminate the necessity of subsequently estimating a large amount of functional obsolescence.

It is imperative that the measure of depreciation be consistent with the cost estimate. It is totally improper to deduct for an item of depreciation or obsolescence that is not "built into" the improvements through the cost estimate. Therefore, the appraiser must know the type of cost estimated and understand the source of the cost data.

Current cost data on modern, functional facilities will be useful in estimating the replacement cost of the subject improvements. If the cost data include some item of obsolescence, even recent factored information will require adjustment before it can be applied to the subject property. Otherwise, the cost of functional obsolescence would theoretically be built into the subject model.

Most contemporary cost manuals are designed to enable the appraiser to estimate cost by component breakdown, unit-in-place, or some physical unit of comparison such as square foot or cubic foot of area. The data in these manuals are usually based on average recent costs of functional buildings. Therefore, the costs analyzed by unit of comparison or unit-in-place will reflect replacement cost, while the segregated cost of components will reflect reproduction cost new. Obviously, caution must be exercised in using cost manuals.

DEPRECIATION AND OBSOLESCENCE

Depreciation is generally defined as a loss in value from all causes, namely, physical deterioration, functional obsolescence, and economic obsolescence.

Physical deterioration is the result of usage and natural forces. Functional obsolescence stems from superadequacies and/or deficiencies inherent in the property. Economic obsolescence is caused by adverse forces or elements outside the property itself.

Physical deterioration and functional obsolescence may be broken down into "curable" and "incurable" items. Economic obsolescence is always incurable as it is beyond the control of the property owner. Curable items of depreciation are measured by the estimated cost to cure. Correction or replacement of items classified as incurable is not considered economically feasible.

Physical Deterioration

Physical deterioration encompasses three categories of depreciation.

1. *Curable: deferred maintenance.* This category includes items of deterioration that should be corrected immediately to preserve the building or to satisfy basic tenancy requirements. The amount of deferred maintenance is the estimated current cost of correcting or curing the problem, e.g., the cost of repairing broken doors and windows, painting interior walls, replacing torn carpet, repairing a leaky roof, or similar problems of inconvenience or undesirability.
2. *Curable: postponed.* These are items of deterioration affecting components that have remaining useful lives and, therefore, should not be replaced at the date of appraisal. The amount of deterioration affecting a short-lived building component is measured as a percentage of the item's estimated cost new on the appraisal date. This percentage is estimated as the relationship between the component's effective age (expired utility in years) and its economic life expectancy if new on the appraisal date. Curable, postponed items of physical deterioration might affect items such as roof cover, wall covering and ornamentation, carpet and other floor covering, water heaters, electrical fixtures, fencing, paving, and other items that will probably require replacement during the remaining useful life of the principal improvements. For example, a roof cover that is eight years old should have an economic life of 20 years if new, but is judged to have a remaining economic life of 15 years. Although its actual age is eight years, its "effective" age is five years (20 – 15) and the accrued depreciation is 25% of the estimated reproduction (or replacement) cost new on the appraisal date.
3. *Incurable physical deterioration.* This factor relates to basic structural components such as the foundation, floor structure, bearing walls, and roof structure, which depreciate completely during the economic life of the structure but cannot be economically corrected so long as the structure has remaining usefulness.

The amount of incurable physical deterioration relates to the effective age of the components and the economic life expectancy of the structure if new. The effective age estimate should be predicated on the assumption that all deferred maintenance items of depreciation have been corrected and a deduction has been made for them.

Presume that the effective age of the subject structure is five years and its economic life, if new, is estimated at 50 years. This would indicate depreciation of 10%. Appraisers may err at this point by failing to recognize that this depreciation affects only the incurable components. If the depreciation factor of 10% is applied to the estimate of total improvement costs, the components previously treated under deferred maintenance and curable postponed deterioration will be depreciated twice. The correct procedure is to multiply the incurable deterioration rate times the estimated cost new of the incurable components. This cost is derived by deducting the estimated cost new of all curable items (before depreciation) from the total estimate of cost new.

The total amount of physical depreciation estimated from all causes should be expressed as a percentage of the reproduction or replacement cost new for future use in the appraisal process.

Functional Obsolescence

Functional obsolescence is a loss in efficiency or utility caused by deficiencies or superadequacies in the building improvements. Deficiencies may be the result of building design or construction, but much obsolescence results from advances in technology that render equipment, fixtures, and other components nonfunctional or inefficient.

Items of functional obsolescence may be either curable or incurable, as determined by their financial feasibility on the appraisal date or within the near future. Throughout the remaining economic life of the improvements, incurable items cause decreased building efficiency, loss of income, or both.

The lack of closets, storage, or bathrooms or a poor floor plan in a residence; inadequate climate control or elevator facilities in office buildings; and deficiencies in electrical capacity, low ceiling clearances and inadequate offices at warehouse facilities are some examples of functional obsolescence. Other examples include narrow corridors in office buildings, obsolete plumbing and lighting fixtures, and superadequacies in wall construction, electrical capacity, or other components.

Inadequate automobile parking and the location of improvements on the site in a configuration that creates inefficiency or loss of utility are also considered functional obsolescence. These will almost invariably be classified as "incurable." For example, consider a building located near the center of a site which economically could be divided into two or more economic units if the improvements were nonexistent. Presuming the improvements have economic value, the functional obsolescence affecting the improvements may be classified as curable or incurable depending on the magnitude of net benefits caused by relocating the improvements. In this instance the entire obsolescence would pertain to the improvements and not to the land because the land value is usually estimated at its optimum use, assumed to be vacant.

There is much controversy about the assessment of functional obsolescence as it relates to cost new. Obsolescence relative to superadequate fixtures, equipment, or other components cannot occur unless the cost of constructing the superadequacy was reflected in reproduction cost new. Estimation of replacement cost would, by definition, have eliminated the superadequacy and precluded the necessity of estimating obsolescence. Measuring functional obsolescence as the entire cost new also would be inaccurate if physical deterioration estimates affecting the obsolete item have already been charged. Therefore, the obsolescence is properly measured as the cost new, less physical deterioration already charged, plus the cost to cure or remove the item.

Functional obsolescence caused by deficiency is measured by the excess cost of constructing or installing the missing item on the appraisal date, as compared with the cost if the item had been installed at the time of original construction. As the item does not exist, no physical deterioration has occurred and none should be charged.

Some functional obsolescence, such as inefficient lighting fixtures, is curable and can be measured as the cost to cure, less physical depreciation previously charged. If the inefficient lighting fixtures are of a design, elegance, or cost which makes it infeasible to cure the obsolescence, the "incurable" obsolescence is properly measured as the cost of the superadequacy, less physical depreciation already charged, plus the discounted present worth of any excess costs of operation, maintenance, and ownership.

It is quite likely that narrow corridors or very high office ceilings are obsolescence items that are incurable—they might be physically curable but prospective increases in net rent probably will not justify the cost of modification plus a reasonable entrepreneurial profit.

A high ceiling is incurable obsolescence measured as the cost of maintaining the excess wall area plus the present worth of the additional utilities and other services required to maintain the space, but minus the physical deterioration estimate previously charged. Excessive wall thickness is a superadequacy, classified as incurable obsolescence, and measured as the reproduction cost new of the excess construction minus the physical deterioration estimate previously charged.

Incurable functional obsolescence such as a poor floor plan, lack of sufficient elevators, or inadequate parking at an office or apartment building is measured as the present worth of the rental loss caused by such inutility. For example, the floor plan and existing elevators will be reflected in the current estimate of cost new, but the parking and elevator deficiencies will not. Presume that market analysis indicates that a functional building with a superior floor plan and adequate elevators will rent for premiums of $.25 and $.50 per square foot per year, respectively. The gross annual rent loss can be converted to an indicated obsolescence by multiplying it by a market-derived gross rent multiplier. Alternatively, the gross rent loss can be adjusted to reflect net annual income for capitalization into indicated obsolescence using various capitalization techniques.

Economic Obsolescence

Economic obsolescence is an incurable loss of improvement value resulting from factors outside the physical property boundaries. This does not mean that the external economic factors are literally incurable, but that they are incurable because the subject ownership has no control over them.

In measuring economic obsolescence, the appraiser must guard against double depreciation—the same economic factors that cause obsolescence and perhaps rent loss to the improvements also affect the underlying land value.

Some examples of economic obsolescence, sometimes called locational obsolescence, include unfavorable odors delivered by prevailing winds, noise and dust from nearby facilities, declining occupancies caused by reduced demand and recessionary trends, and increasing fixed and operating expenses, particularly taxes and utilities.

The economic factors are obviously incurable and may be national or international in scope. The specific local sources of this type of obsolescence are also incurable unless the noise, dust, and odors violate zoning or governmental regulations.

Economic obsolescence may be measured by comparing properties affected by the detrimental influence with similar properties that are not affected. The apparent rent loss caused by the detrimental factor is then capitalized using a gross rent multiplier or an appropriate net income capitalization technique. The capitalized value loss relates to the total property and must be adjusted because economic obsolescence relates only to the improvements. The impact of the detrimental factors presumably is reflected in the land value estimate, and failure to adjust the loss would result in double depreciation.

The adjustment can be appropriately made by multiplying the total apparent value loss by the market-observed ratio of improvement value to total property value for similar properties in the area. If the apparent net rent loss is $1,000 per year, the appropriate capitalization rate is 10%, and improvements typically represent 80% of property value, the estimate of economic obsolescence affecting the improvements is calculated $1,000 \div .10 \times .80 = \$8,000$.

Estimating economic obsolescence resulting from oversupply or depressed economic conditions is somewhat more complex. In such situations, it is quite likely that the cost approach will not be a reliable value indicator, but will reflect a condition of economic infeasibility. The difference between the value indications by the income and sales comparison approaches and those produced by the cost approach, which reflect only physical depreciation and functional obsolescence, will be the implied economic obsolescence.

An example of economic obsolescence is an apartment complex which is vacant or experiencing low occupancy because of a lack of effective demand or unit oversupply within the specific market. This condition could apply to proposed construction as well as existing projects. The appraiser will be concerned with market factors such as existing and proposed unit inventory, historical and current absorption, occupancy levels, and rental rates. These factors are significant in validating projections of absorption, occupancies, and rents for the specific subject property.

Presume that it is expected to take three years for the project to attain stabilization of occupancy producing 90% of the market rent potential. The amount of economic obsolescence attributable to oversupply is the present worth of the net income loss throughout the absorption or occupancy stabilization period. This factor will be used for adjustment in all of the value approaches utilized by the appraiser.

ADDITIONAL COMMENTS ON DEPRECIATION

The preceding discussion outlines various procedures for measuring the value loss resulting from specific factors. The sum of the observed estimates of depreciation and obsolescence, and the resulting estimates of depreciated cost new, should be confirmed by market analysis if at all possible.

The market method of depreciation analysis begins by allocating part of the sale price of each comparable property to land value and the balance to the improvements. If the land value allocation is based on an analysis of competitive land sales, the improvement price allocation essentially reflects a depreciated cost as perceived by market participants on the date of sale. It is then necessary to estimate the cost of replacement or reproduction of the improvements as of the date of sale. The difference between the estimated cost new and the implied improvement price is the total depreciation indicated by the market at the date of sale. For purposes of market depreciation analysis, it is important that the land value and cost new estimates relate to the dates of the respective market transactions.

The total market-implied depreciation for each sale can be further analyzed into a percentage of cost new and the depreciation of principal improvements per year of actual age, expressed in dollars or as an annual percentage. The analyst may elect to report these observations on a straight-line or sinking-fund/annuity basis.

The rate of observed depreciation can serve as a foundation for projecting the remaining economic life of the subject improvements, a significant factor in completing a valuation utilizing the sales comparison and income approaches. In the sales comparison approach, adjustments for age/condition and remaining utility depend heavily on this type of analysis. The capitalization method and technique and the rate of recapture (anticipated future depreciation) selected depend on the appraiser's observations regarding the remaining economic life of the improvements, expressed as of the appraisal date.

The remaining economic life implied by sales data analysis, plus the actual age, suggest the total useful life of the sale improvements if new. The following example summarizes the process.

A retail store building containing 4,250 sq. ft. of gross area was constructed 42 years ago on a site containing 8,250 sq. ft. The property recently sold for $34,000, or $8.00 per sq. ft. of gross building area, including land and improvements. The land value is estimated on the date of sale at $2.06 per sq. ft., or $17,000. The improvement price, therefore, is approximately $17,000.

The reproduction cost new of the improvements is estimated at $72,200, or approximately $17.00 per sq. ft. Accordingly, the difference between the $72,200 cost new and the $17,000 improvement price at the time of sale indicates total depreciation of $55,200 or 76.4% of cost new. The total depreciation of 76.4% suggests an annual straight-line depreciation rate of 1.8% (76.4% ÷ 42 years of actual age). By extrapolation, the 1.8% rate indicates that the improvements, if new, would have a life expectancy of approximately 55 years (100% ÷ 1.8%).

MULTIPLE IMPROVEMENTS

An economic unit comprised of multiple, but complementary, improvements which vary significantly in age and condition frequently poses difficulties in the estimation of depreciation. A truck terminal facility with several buildings and related site improvements may be designed and situated to be reasonably functional for the intended usage. Yet, the four buildings differ substantially in age and significance to the overall operational entity. The principal building is a 35-year-old terminal. Two less significant, but important, buildings are the office and truck garage buildings which are each about 20 years old. There is a fourth building that doubles as a truck wash and houses the scale pit; it is smaller and only five years old.

Each of the subject buildings might have a presumed economic life estimate of 40 years, if new and located separately on proper economic sites, or if new and all located on the same site. Therefore, it might appear that the remaining economic life of the terminal is five years, and the useful lives of the other buildings range from 20 to 35 years.

It would be illogical, however, to conclude that the three newer, but less significant, buildings have remaining economic lives extending beyond the economic life of the principal improvement. Theoretically, the principal building will no longer exist when its economic life expires. It is quite possible, however, that the remaining life of the principal improvement might be extended for several years due to the existence of the complementary improvements. It would be totally improper in most situations to evaluate the remaining useful lives and observed depreciation of the individual buildings without considering the utility of all the buildings as a single economic unit.

USEFUL LIFE VS. ECONOMIC LIFE

Many appraisers think the terms *useful life* and *economic life* are synonymous and interchangeable. This is erroneous and there are several notable reasons why they differ.

Economic life is the period during which the improvements on the specific site are capable of producing enough net operating income to yield a fair return on the land value. At the point in time when there is insufficient net income to provide a return on the land, a prudent owner will consider demolition of the existing improvements and redevelopment of the site. This situation could conceivably result when a relatively modern building is located in an area that is experiencing rapid land value appreciation or where the availability of land is scarce and the site will be redeveloped for a more profitable use.

Economic life is a function of economic viability, while useful life denotes the period over which a facility can be competitive and functional for use as designed. A new, modern office building may be expected to serve the needs of the typical office tenant or occupant for many years and therefore have a long useful life. At the same time the improvements may not be capable of producing a net income sufficient to satisfy the reasonable return requirements of the land. The remaining useful life would apparently be extensive, but the site is not developed to its optimum use and economic life would have expired.

Valuation Conclusion through Reconciliation

To conclude the valuation process, the appraiser reviews the property rights appraised in light of the economic principles applied through one or more of the valuation approaches. Most professional appraisers do not consider reconciliation to be an averaging of value indications, nor is it the selection of the value indicated by the approach most preferred by the appraiser. Instead, the appraiser weighs the strengths and weaknesses of all the estimates and projections formulated in the valuation process and rejects those that are contrary to observed market phenomena. Accordingly, the final value estimate will not usually be equal to any one of the specific value indications or their arithmetic average.

A secondary, but important, part of the reconciliation process is the allocation of the final value estimate according to legal and financial interests and physical assets. These might be categorized:

1. Legal—leased fee, leasehold, or easements.
2. Financial—mortgage and equity components.
3. Physical—Land and improvements (certain real property valuations may also include an allocation of furniture, fixtures, and equipment).

The physical value allocation is typically made with the land valued according to its optimum use, presumed to be vacant as of the date of the appraisal. It is important that the appraiser value the land at its optimum use and that the treatment of economic and functional obsolescence affecting the improvements is consistent with that use. It may also be desirable to estimate land value for total value allocation according to the site's present usage. This method of allocation could help determine the significance of the special-use value of the improvements and might be useful in estimating the effect a particular event or project might have on the land, improvements, and type of operations.

Violation of the consistent use theory, where the land is appraised at its optimum use and the improvements are valued according to their present use, can usually be avoided if the preceding processes are followed.

The final value estimate can be used to test the highest and best use of the site by analyzing the final property value in fee simple into value per square foot, front foot, acre, or other unit of comparison. If the indicated value units exceed the range of land prices exhibited by market data, then the subject improvements apparently contribute to the overall value and confirm that the highest and best use of the property is as presently improved.

The final value estimate can also be analyzed into value indications per square foot of building area, inclusive or exclusive of land value. Such value allocations and analyses may be quite useful in establishing the magnitude of depreciation or obsolescence affecting the improvements. The final determination of depreciation affecting the improvements cannot be made until the reconciliation process and final value estimations have been completed.

Some appraisers avoid using certain value approaches, capitalization methods, or techniques and try to justify this in their reports by stating, "Investors do not use this method," or "this technique," or "this approach." Such an observation is not surprising as most investors are not trained in the rudiments of appraising. Investors make decisions in an attempt to reach specific financial or personal goals. Frequently, these decisions are not based on an analysis of the activities of others in the marketplace. Investors may consider only supply and demand for similar properties, available mortgage funds, and other general economic factors that influence prices and terms.

The appraiser is an observer of the market and the many economic factors that influence value. Accordingly, professional appraisers must use any and all available processes that will help them analyze the market and derive supportable value conclusions. Each method, technique, and approach is somewhat significant in most appraisal assignments and the appraiser should consider each one an aid in solving the problem.

The astute and successful investor or developer may base decisions on criteria which differ from the criteria of other successful investors. The market is made up of successful and unsuccessful investors. The appraiser employs analytic processes and techniques totally unfamiliar to typical investors which may reveal degrees of consistency or inconsistency within the market. This observation alone might be the most significant aspect of the entire valuation process.

In the value analysis, which culminates with the reconciliation, the appraiser should be satisfied that a prudent investor, armed with the facts presented, familiar with the methods of detailed analysis, and aware of various investment alternatives (via the value approaches), would probably arrive at the same value/price conclusion.

Most buyers and sellers are not as knowledgeable or as prudent as the prevailing definition of market value presumes. Unless the appraiser assumes that the parties are knowledgeable concerning the value techniques, methods, and processes presented by appraisers, it cannot be anticipated that all valuation principles and value factors have been considered. If they have not been considered, the investment decision may not be a prudent one. Nevertheless, the appraiser is charged with estimating a prudently negotiated, probable price which can legitimately and logically be labelled "market value."

Special Valuation and Analysis Problems

Section 3 is a compendium of somewhat unrelated chapters dealing with a variety of valuation problems. The objective of this section is to address many, but obviously not all, situations involving special valuation and analysis problems. These subjects are frequently the bases for disagreement among appraisers and such controversy leads to value divergencies.

Several of the chapters offer observations and points of view, but no conclusions. The author recognizes that controversy abounds among appraisers and others who are concerned with value judgments. The author's viewpoints are presented to provoke thought and discussion, which may result in a learning experience.

Valuation of Special-Use Property Types

SPECIAL-USE VS. LIMITED-MARKET FACILITIES

The appraisal of special-use property types is often the subject of controversy. Occasionally, limited-market properties are inappropriately classified as special-purpose although a limited but confirmed market exists.

Most improvements, including office and apartment buildings, are designed for a specific use or occupancy and may appear to be special purpose because they are more functional and profitable when used in accordance with their design. The term *special purpose* or *special use,* however, is interpreted by appraisers to denote a significant distinction between generally accepted or typical properties and those that are unusual and have few possible users or owners.

Special-use properties exist in public, quasi-public, industrial, religious, institutional, and private sectors. Certain property types such as schools, hospitals, cemeteries, and recreational facilities appear to be special-use facilities but actually may be operated for anticipated profit and are more accurately classified as limited-market facilities.

The appraiser of an unusual property type must first determine if the facility is limited market or truly special use. If there are enough sales or lease data to suggest that a reasonably active market for continued use does exist, then the property is more appropriately classified as limited market. On the other hand, if this property type seldom leases or sells, it would likely be considered special use.

This essay originally appeared in the July 1980 issue of *The Appraisal Journal.*

VALUATION CONSIDERATIONS AND PROCESSES

Appraisers of special-use properties are usually faced with numerous potential difficulties which defy market analysis and value justification. Consequently, the term *value in use* has evolved as an acceptable substitute for market value as just compensation in eminent domain proceedings involving special-use properties. Appraisers of limited-market properties are justified in using all valuation approaches that appropriately reflect investor attitudes towards the market for that property type.

Appraisers traditionally have concluded that the cost approach is the only approach of significance in valuing special-use properties. As was discussed in Section 2, the cost approach involves adding the market value of the land, assumed to be vacant, to the replacement or reproduction cost new of the improvements minus depreciation. This approach is fraught with weakness and poses particular problems in properly estimating land value and measuring observed estimates and types of depreciation in special-use properties.

For example, a specialty manufacturing enterprise may enjoy substantial benefits due to its strategic location near distribution centers or because of the special characteristics of the structure. If distribution methods change drastically or technological advances in the industry cause functional obsolescence in the subject building, it is apparent that value in use will decline accordingly. Therefore, it is quite conceivable that functional and economic obsolescence, coupled with physical deterioration, could make a facility totally unacceptable to the industry. Accordingly, the improvements would have no measurable value in use and the entire value would be inherent in the land.

In such instances, analyses of land value plus estimated cost new, less certain depreciation (perhaps physical depreciation and some functional or economic obsolescence), might not reflect a realistic indication of value in use. It is of utmost importance to understand and relate functional and economic obsolescence in all appraisals of value in use.

LAND VALUATION AND ECONOMIC OBSOLESCENCE

A major decision confronting the appraiser of special-use property is whether to estimate first the value of the land as if vacant and available for redevelopment to its highest and best use, or the value of the land consistent with existing land use. This decision will affect the appraiser's estimate of depreciation from all causes, including functional and economic obsolescence.

The market value of the land, if vacant and available for development to its optimum use, could exceed the value of the site for its committed use. Land values at the specific location may have increased substantially, yet the special-use activity could function as efficiently on a less expensive, alternative site. If the site is committed, prudent ownership will most likely maintain occupancy of the existing facility until the improvements are no longer functional or until land value increases so much that demolition of the improvements is justified.

The difference between land value at optimum use of the site and land value for the subject use on an "ideal" site is economic obsolescence. If the cost approach is properly processed, this item of obsolescence will be reflected as a deduction from the estimated cost new of the improvements.

If the subject site is valued consistent with the committed use, land value will be less, eliminating the necessity to estimate and deduct economic obsolescence from cost new. The value-in-use estimates using the alternative processes should be essentially identical.

The appraiser must be careful in estimating depreciation from physical, functional, and economic causes in special-use properties. Physical deterioration is appropriately estimated using age-life methods and analysis of costs to cure deferred maintenance items.

The valuation of special-use properties with the cost approach should reflect any functional obsolescence caused by superadequacies or deficiencies of a functional nature, relative to the type and use of the facilities. The remaining useful life of a special-purpose facility may be influenced by technological advances and trends in the specific industry for which the facility is adapted. Functional obsolescence caused by these advances should be deducted if either reproduction or replacement cost new of the improvements is estimated.

Remember that the estimate of reproduction cost new assumes reproduction of a facsimile facility while replacement cost new replaces utility without consideration of functional superadequacies or deficiencies. Accordingly, superadequacies cannot be properly deducted from replacement cost new, but must be deducted from reproduction cost new. Estimates of replacement cost new will not necessarily reflect technological changes in the specific industry; it is more proper to deduct the relative obsolescences from replacement cost new in such instances.

Economic obsolescence affecting special-use improvements has already been discussed and in most instances may be defined as the difference between the estimate of land value if vacant and available for development to its optimum use, and the estimate of land value if the specific improvements were theoretically located on an ideal, alternative site.

The following case study is offered to clarify these processes:

A reasonably modern church facility, built approximately 10 years ago, is located on a 20-acre site in a commercially developing area. The appraiser determines that this is truly a special-purpose facility because prospective sale prices that would impute real value to the improvements are extremely difficult to obtain. The church is located in a sectarian neighborhood and a public agency is acquiring it under threat of condemnation.

These observations lead the appraiser to conclude that another denomination or religious order would not be highly motivated to acquire this facility if it were available for purchase. Having concluded that just compensation is more appropriately reflected by value in use than by market value, the first step is land valuation. Market evidence strongly suggests that the land, if vacant, would sell for $25,000 per acre, or $500,000. However, an equally desirable 20-acre church site within a few blocks was recently acquired by another congregation for $10,000 per acre, or $200,000. For purposes of the value in use appraisal, should the subject land value be estimated at $10,000 or $25,000 per acre?

Perhaps this question can only be answered after the appraiser resolves the questions regarding cost new and depreciation. If the 10-year-old building includes construction excesses such as superadequate walls or excessive ceiling heights, it may be more proper to estimate replacement cost new to eliminate inclusion of these items of functional obsolescence in the cost estimate.

The question of depreciation can be expanded to include all forms and types of depreciation. If all types of physical deterioration are deducted from cost new, the estimate of incurable physical deterioration must relate to some estimate of remaining economic life; this strongly suggests that the building will ultimately expire economically. If this is true, any economic obsolescence should also be deducted. The estimate of economic obsolescence will be the "excess" land value of $300,000, which represents the difference between the land value if vacant and the land value for the specific improvement type if constructed on the proper economic site.

If identical improvements are theoretically in place on the two sites, the estimates of value in use will be identical, although the value allocation to land and improvements may be substantially different. Value in use will necessarily be the same if either facility can adequately and sufficiently accommodate the congregation. The following table summarizes possible analyses of these facilities.

Paying more than $1,000,000 for Property A would violate the consistent use theory. If only physical deterioration were deducted, the building would theoretically never expire; the owner would be paid for increasing land

	Property A		Property B	
Site value				
(20 acres each)		$ 500,000		$ 200,000
Building cost new	$1,000,000		$1,000,000	
Less depreciation				
Physical	(100,000)		(100,000)	
Functional	(100,000)		(100,000)	
Economic	(300,000)		(—)	
Depreciated cost		500,000		800,000
Indicated				
value in use		$1,000,000		$1,000,000

value and slowly depreciating building cost, although the building might not represent the proper use of the site. Property B is just as capable of satisfying the church owners' needs as Property A, and it is incumbent upon the appraiser to estimate a fair value in use to ensure that the owners are paid just compensation.

The appraiser should be alert to professional requirements and clarify the purpose and function of the appraisal of limited-market and special-use property types. Erroneous classification of a limited-market property as a special-use property might lead the appraiser to rely on the cost approach when market data are available for analysis.

It is quite possible for the market value of a special-use property to exceed its value in use, but such a conclusion requires a thorough understanding of industry needs regarding buildings, equipment, and improvements. The critical question in appraising value in use is the degree to which the specific improvements serve the needs of the business/industry at the specific location. Technological advances in the industry, the functionality of the improvements, changes in the market for the industry's product, and the economics of the specific location should all be considered.

Use of Cash Equivalency in Valuation

The definition of market value, which was discussed earlier, anticipates a sale reflecting financing terms and conditions prevalent in the market at the date of appraisal. If the prevailing market reflects cash transactions, then market value and cash value will be synonymous.

Frequently, however, an estimate of market value under typical terms will not assist the client in making a decision or solving the immediate problem. Nevertheless, the estimate of market value may be a logical beginning for further analysis of cash equivalency or cash value.

There are many possible applications of cash equivalency estimates in real estate circumstances, including:

1. Analysis of price data in speculative markets to derive a more consistent price pattern for decision-making.
2. Extrapolation of value indications, with a variety of prices and financing terms, from cash equivalent prices.
3. Establishment of ad valorem assessments and taxes.
4. Computation of estate taxes.
5. Estimation of just compensation for eminent domain proceedings.
6. Calculation of the market value of notes secured by real property.

Cash equivalency estimates may not currently be applicable in certain circumstances or permissible in certain jurisdictions, but their possible uses are discussed here to provoke thought.

CASH EQUIVALENCY IN VALUING SPECULATIVE PROPERTIES

The appraiser of speculative properties, particularly rural and suburban acreage, may observe numerous transactions and listings with acreage prices and financing terms that reflect no discernible pattern on which to base reasonable value conclusions. Sellers are frequently motivated to accept a higher price, which will ultimately be taxed at capital gains rates, in lieu of higher interest rates, which are taxed at less favorable, ordinary income rates.

The appraiser may readily determine that any sale of similar acreage in this market area will require substantial seller financing for a major part of the purchase price. Determination of typical terms and price may be a practical impossibility. Converting each of the transaction prices to a cash equivalent price will provide additional insight into the market and probably produce a more consistent pattern of prices. These cash equivalent prices can then be compared with the subject property to derive a subject value estimate of cash equivalency. This cash equivalency can be the basis for computing, by extrapolation, a range of specific market value indications under a variety of assumptions regarding down payments, interest rates, and amortization periods.

The following data are presented to illustrate the calculation of cash equivalencies for sale properties and their application to the valuation of the subject property.

Sale 1 is a 100-acre tract that sold three months ago for $100,000, or $1,000 per acre. The purchaser paid $50,000, or 50% of the purchase price, in cash at closing and the seller financed the balance. The note requires the payment of principal plus interest at 9% per annum throughout a seven-year amortization period. Payments of $9,934.53 are due at the end of each year.

Sale 2 is a 90-acre tract that sold last month for $108,000, or $1,200 per acre, with the seller financing $81,000, or 75% of the price, for a 15-year period. The note requires the payment of principal plus 8.5% annual interest at the end of each year. Annual debt service is $9,754.06.

Sale 3 is a 125-acre tract that sold last month for $187,500, or $1,500 per acre, with the seller financing $178,125 or 95% of the purchase price for a 25-year term at an annual interest rate of 8%. The note prescribes payment of interest, calculated at $14,250 per year, for 10 years; debt service, including amortization of principal plus interest, or $20,810.26 per year, is payable over the following 15 years.

Calculating cash equivalency involves converting each respective note to its cash equivalent and adding the cash down payment to produce an indicated "cash equivalent" price for each transaction. The investor in a note secured by real estate will pay a price which represents the present worth of the right to receive the periodic payments of principal and interest.

The discount/interest rate applicable to the note will be selected with consideration for the relative degree of equity and investment security, the payment schedule, the credit-worthiness of the mortgagor, and the yield prospects of alternative investment opportunities. Ideally, the appraiser will have sufficient data to abstract discount rates from known sales of similar notes. In the absence of such data, a judgment call is necessary.

Presume that the first security mortgages applicable to the three sales above demand a 13% annual discount rate when applied to the respective debt-service payments. The cash equivalent prices are computed below, utilizing present worth factors and end-of-period payments.

Present Worth Calculations		Cash Equivalent Price	
		Total	Per Acre
Sale 1 Equity	$50,000		
Debt service ($9,934.53 × 4.4226*)	43,936	$93,936	$939
Sale 2 Equity	$27,000		
Debt service ($9,754.06 × 6.4624**)	63,035	$90,035	$1,000
Sale 3 Equity	$9,375		
Debt service ($14,250 × 5.4262***)	77,323		
$20,810.26 × 1.9037****	39,616	$126,314	$1,011

*Present worth or annuity factor for payment of $1 at end of each year for 7 years, discounted at 13% per annum.
**Annuity factor for 15 years, discounted at 13% per annum.
***Annuity factor for 10 years, discounted at 13% per annum.
****Annuity factor for 15 years, deferred 10 years, discounted at 13% per annum.

The appraiser might conclude from this analysis that the cash equivalent value of the subject acreage is $1,000 per acre. The unadjusted acreage prices differed by 50%, ranging from $1,000 to $1,500; they were adjusted to a more narrow 6% range from $939 to $1,011 per acre. With the cash equivalent value of the price reasonably supported, the probable price reflecting an assortment of interest rates, mortgage ratios, and payback periods can be calculated by extrapolation using algebraic formulae or simple arithmetic.

Sale 3 is analyzed algebraically to illustrate the process and test the hypothesis that the cash equivalent equals the present worth of all equity and debt-service cash flows when discounted at selected note yield or discount rates. The value being tested is 67.4% of price. Present worth factors in the following formula correspond to those used in the cash equivalency analysis of the sale.

Where CEV = cash equivalent value and P = price.

CEV = .05P + .95P(.08) (5.4262) + .95P(.1168) (1.9037)
CEV = .05P + .4124P + .2112P
CEV = .6736P, or 67.4%

Of course, dollars of discount and price could be substituted for the pertinent symbols to derive the same confirmations.

Pricing by Extrapolation: An Example

The appraiser is to estimate a reasonable price for the current sale of a 150-acre tract in the same general area as the three market transactions analyzed above. The seller insists on an installment sale with less than 30% down for income tax purposes and, although aware of acreage prices in the area, the seller is motivated by pride to insist on a price greater than any known transactions for similar acreage.

The seller will finance 70% of the price for a 30-year term. Only interest at 6% per annum will be payable at the end of each of the first seven years. Interest-only payments will increase to reflect 7.5% per year during the next five years. Principal, plus 8% interest, will be payable over the following 18 years. Assume that a prudent note investor would expect a 13% annual rate of return. As value and price are unknown, it is not possible to determine the face value of the note or the debt service.

The problem can be solved by using an algebraic formulation if discount or value is sought, or by using dollars when testing for the reasonableness of the price.

CEV = .30P(1.00) + .70P(.06) (4.4226) + .70P(.075) (1.4950) + .70P(.1067)
(1.5781)
CEV = .30P + .1857P + .0785P + .1179P
CEV = .6821P, or 68.21%

If the analysis of sales suggests a cash equivalency of $1,000 per acre, the indicated price for the acreage with these sample terms will be calculated:

$1,000 ÷ .6821 = $1,466 per acre

If either the seller or the buyer insists on different terms, payback periods, or equity payments at closing, the factors in the formula will differ and different price discounts will result. The appraiser/analyst should be aware of certain factors such as excessive prices and debt-to-value ratios, which may well produce higher note discount rates.

Although the seller is willing to sell the land at $1,466 per acre, investigation reveals that the typical investor in the note expects a yield of 18% per annum because of the long-term nature of the investment. The required acreage investment price can be recalculated to satisfy the note investor and provide the same cash equivalency to the property owner, although it might not be satisfactory to the prospective purchaser of the real property.

The price under this alternative is calculated:

$$CEV = .30P(1.00) + .70P(.06)(3.8115) + .70P(.075)(.9817)$$
$$+ .70P(.1067)(.7236)$$
$$CEV = .30P + .1601P + .0515P + .0540P$$
$$CEV = .5656P, \text{ or } 56.56\% \text{ of price}$$

To provide a $1,000 cash equivalency, the property will be priced as follows:

$$\$1,000 \div .5656 = \$1,768 \text{ per acre}$$

SPECIAL APPLICATIONS OF CASH EQUIVALENCY

Ad valorem taxes, estate taxes, and just compensation in eminent domain matters are frequently computed on the basis of prevalent "favorable" financing terms. Speculative acreage and some income properties probably will not sell for cash, but the probable prices still can be converted into their cash equivalents. It is illogical to pay increased taxes on fictitious "value" created by intangible financing. The price may well have been exorbitant because of the seller's desire to defer taxes or to obtain a low interest rate over an extended period. Similarly, a public agency should not be required to pay an inflated price, based on financing peculiarities, when property rights are to be acquired by the agency with cash.

Appraisers will most likely disagree in valuation matters if they hold different assumptions as to the effect of high-leverage financing terms. Cash equivalency balances these differences so that the appraiser can express value conclusions under a multitude of presumed or stated conditions. The process and calculations can be useful in supporting comparative adjustments produced by the sales comparison approach and in negotiation counseling of buyers and sellers. They may also be beneficial to attorneys involved with eminent domain and domestic cases involving real property.

Expressing Value Estimates in Constant vs. Current Dollars

The definition of market value typically cited by appraisers suggests that the value estimate is expressed as the amount of money that a property should bring on the appraisal date. However, appraisers sometimes project cash flow escalations and value appreciation due to inflation over the anticipated marketing or ownership period. This is a major inconsistency that could result in erroneous value conclusions unless discount or capitalization rates that reflect the additional risks of inflation (purchasing-power risk) are used to balance the equation.

It is the author's contention that the market value definition demands that value must be expressed in terms of the current purchasing power of the dollar on the appraisal date. It is readily apparent that future prices may well reflect more dollars, but the purchasing power of those dollars may be considerably lower. Derivation of market value estimates often requires the projection of revenue and expenses many years hence.

Constant dollars are dollars that are adjusted for inflation or deflation to yield relatively constant purchasing power. Conversely, the term "current dollars" indicates face value without regard to purchasing power. For example, average unit values of $50,000 in 1958 might equate to approximately $100,000 in terms of 1970 dollars. Therefore, $100,000 in 1970 would buy a "constant dollar" or equivalent amount of goods as $50,000 would have purchased in 1958.

These distinctions in nomenclature and philosophy are of primary importance to the appraiser who makes decisions regarding future rents, expenses, and resale prices; capitalization rates; and the effects on yield of amortizing a mortgage with "cheaper" dollars.

If the appraisal problem involves a conventional property type in which

1) rents and expenses can be readily estimated in terms of present dollars, 2) the property is reasonably stabilized as to occupancy and rent levels, and 3) the existing market rates for income capitalization can reasonably be ascertained, then current value estimation is rather routine.

However, major difficulties may arise when the appraisal problem involves a property which will require several years to complete and market or a large, income-producing complex which will require several years to lease to reasonable expectations. The appraiser has at least two options in the valuation of such properties: to project revenue and expenses in terms of constant dollars or in terms of current (inflated) dollars. The only certainty is present purchasing power, therefore, any projection of increased revenue due to inflation should be offset by an increase in risk, reflected in an increased discount rate. If the increased revenue is projected as a result of increasing demand rather than inflationary pressures, the present market rate will be most appropriate.

The true test for the appraiser is the range of discount rates observed in the market for similar and competitive investments. The investor anticipating value appreciation because of increased demand or inflation will likely pay a price which, properly and thoroughly analyzed, will reflect a lower discount or capitalization rate if constant dollars are projected. If current (inflated) dollars are projected for revenue and expenses, a higher discount rate will likely be observed.

CASE STUDY

An office building containing 100,000 sq. ft. of rentable area is currently capable of producing a gross annual rent of $1,000,000, and total expenses are projected at $500,000 during the first year. Market studies and historical trends suggest that revenue should increase by compounding at 10% per year, while expenses should increase by 15% per year during the anticipated 10-year holding period. Therefore, projected revenue and expenses are summarized in the accompanying table.

The property is presently under contract for sale at a price of $5,000,000, in cash. If the constant dollar net income of $500,000 (Year 1) is related to price, the overall capitalization rate equals 10.0%. If current dollars are used, the overall rates will vary each year from 10% to 12.37%, and average 11.57%. The average 1.57% increase in the overall capitalization rate is apparently the rate applicable to purchasing-power risk.

If the subject property is analyzed in a manner consistent with the method for rate derivation from data analysis, then the value conclusion

Year	Revenue	Expenses	Net Income	Change in Net Income
1	$ 1,000,000	$ 500,000	$ 500,000	—
2	1,100,000	575,000	525,000	+ 5.00%
3	1,210,000	661,250	548,750	+ 4.52
4	1,331,000	760,438	570,562	+ 3.97
5	1,464,100	874,503	589,597	+ 3.34
6	1,610,510	1,005,678	604,832	+ 2.58
7	1,771,561	1,156,530	615,031	+ 1.69
8	1,948,717	1,330,010	618,707	+ 0.60
9	2,143,589	1,529,511	614,078	– 0.75
10	2,357,948	1,758,938	599,010	– 2.46
Total	$15,937,425	$10,151,858	$5,785,567	
Average	$ 1,593,742	$ 1,015,186	$ 578,557	+ 15.71%

should be plausible. However, valuation errors frequently occur when escalated net income projections are capitalized at the current-dollar, market-supported rate. The average projected net income of $578,557 reflects an overall rate of 11.57% at the contract price of $5,000,000. Using the average net income of $578,557 and a market-derived rate of 10% will suggest a justifiable price or value of $5,785,000, which exceeds the actual price by $785,000, or 15.7%.

The preceding scenario illustrates the danger of projecting escalating revenue and expenses with resulting net income estimates discounted to present worth using rates derived from constant-dollar sales analysis.

Discounting Deferred Expenditures

The valuation of properties involving demolition costs or restoration of the premises upon lease expiration or completion of public improvements frequently prompts the appraiser to consider the propriety of discounting deferred expenditures. Two examples are presented to illustrate this problem.

Example 1. Assume that a leased facility is expected to be vacated when the lease expires several years hence. If the premises are leased to a strong credit firm with the provision that the lessee is responsible for removing specialty fixtures and additions and restoring the premises to accommodate typical use, the appraisal problem may be minimized. If the problem involves estimation of the value of the leased fee interest, the discount rate for capitalization will be selected with consideration for the risks of collection and satisfaction of all other lease provisions, including building restoration.

Estimation of fee simple value ignores the impact of the current lease and essentially assumes that the lessee has relocated. If the appraiser, in estimating the market value of fee simple ownership, anticipates that the lessor/owner is responsible for removing the specialty items and restoring the space, a decision must be made as to how to treat the costs to cure.

A reliable contractor has provided an estimate of the current cost of removal and restoration. Discounting this estimate before deducting it from the stabilized current value of the property would be erroneous because the unadjusted value and the current cost to cure are both expressed in terms of current dollars and, therefore, do not need to be discounted further. Simply subtracting the anticipated current cost to cure from the current stabilized value should reflect a plausible estimate of market value.

Example 2. Shopping center improvements located on a very desirable site on a major thoroughfare are judged to have no value in an economic sense, but they do have substantial interim-use value as the site probably will be redeveloped in approximately five years when major road and transit station improvements are completed. The estimates of land value, interim improvement value, and current demolition costs are strongly supportable. The accuracy of the current market value estimate depends on whether or not the demolition cost estimate is discounted for the five-year interim period.

As in the preceding example, all value and cost estimates are expressed in terms of present worth; therefore, further discounting of demolition costs would be improper. If the contractor/estimator had been asked to express the anticipated costs several years hence, it would have been absolutely necessary to discount those costs to present worth before deducting them from stabilized value to produce plausible market value estimates.

Another possible method, which is not recommended because of projection hazards, is to estimate probable future value and deduct future restoration/demolition costs. The net future value will then be discounted to present worth, i.e., market value.

Valuation of Individual Parcels in Assemblage

The valuation of an economic site created by assemblage presents a simple problem in comparison with the valuation of individual parcels that are relatively unmarketable without assemblage.

The market value of an individual parcel may be reasonably estimated by observing market transactions within the subject vicinity. Market analyses may reveal that most of the activity in areas of transitional land use reflects speculation as to future use. This could be a clue as to the probability of assemblage. A larger site may be redeveloped to optimize the land asset, changing the highest and best use from speculative holding to a more lucrative and marketable product.

The valuation problem depends to some degree on the general awareness that the assemblage program has begun. A prudent owner or appraiser/consultant with this awareness would consider the nature of the anticipated development, the reputation of the developer/agent, and the other parcels and ownership entities involved to assess the probability of a successful assemblage. The value of each parcel will likely depend on its size, frontage, topography, and location within the proposed assemblage. Therefore, it is of utmost importance that key parcels be acquired in title or by purchase options early in the assemblage effort.

If the assemblage program is common knowledge or can be readily deduced with reasonable research, estimating the value of a single parcel may be quite a challenge. If the individual parcel is improved, its marketability and corresponding market value may be readily estimated from sales analysis of individual properties with similar current use. However, the more immediate question is the parcel's value to the land assembler. Accordingly, the value estimate may be better expressed as "special value" or "value as part of assemblage," rather than market value. If this or another assemblage is inevitable, the highest and best use may conclusively be speculative holding for assemblage, and the estimate of market value will reflect these probabilities.

Substantial divergencies in value estimates for such properties may occur, particularly when equally competent and professional appraisers or consultants differ in their evaluation of: 1) the importance of the individual parcel to the assemblage, 2) the present status or probability of completing the assemblage, 3) the prospective timing of assemblage, and 4) the concept of market value as opposed to warranted or justifiable price.

If the parcel is not strategic or critical to the assemblage, unreasonable price demands by the owner may influence the developer to exclude the parcel or reduce the scale of the assemblage/development. As the assemblage nears completion, the value of the remaining parcels to the developer almost always increases unless the parcel has marginal utility to the project. The prudent, experienced assembler anticipates some "holdout" owners who demand premium prices. The effect of such holdouts on the overall price is usually negligible, as the prices of larger and more critical parcels have usually been established much earlier. Market studies and other planning efforts probably will eliminate most surprises that could hamper the completion of a properly conceived land assemblage.

A major valuation problem is the allocation of plottage value to individual parcels. For example, a large assemblage involving 25 homeowners in an area in transition to commercial use is contemplated, and the assembled tract will be redeveloped into a large-scale commercial project. The individual parcels differ substantially in lot size, building size, age, and condition; several have greater marketability or development potential with or without the envisioned assemblage. Should each owner receive a consistent, average price per square foot of land or should the prime sites command premiums? What adjustment should be made, if any, for a parcel that has no improvements, has little or no street frontage, or is partially encumbered with easements?

The first task will be to evaluate each individual parcel at its respective highest and best use. It is quite possible that the buildings have contributory value and that some are more valuable than others. The market value of the entire assembled site will then be estimated. Presumably, the assembled site will have a greater market value than the sum of the individual market value estimates. If this is not so, assemblage would usually be considered illogical.

A possible resolution would be to allocate total assemblage value or price on the basis of the percentaged relationship between the market value of the individual parcel and the sum of the market value estimates before assemblage. For example, if a parcel is valued at $100,000 before assemblage, and the sum of the value estimates for the 25 parcels to be assembled is $3,000,000, then the subject parcel represents 3.33% of the total market value estimate.

Further assume that the assembled tract has a market value—or perhaps even a signed contract or offer—of $5,000,000. If all of the parcels are necessary for the proposed development, each part of the assemblage may have reasonably equivalent value upon completion of the assemblage. Accordingly, the reasonable value of the sample parcel might be allocated as 3.33% of the $5,000,000 assemblage value, or $166,500.

Another method for deriving value indications for individual parcels in a prospective assemblage is a comparative analysis of the apparent or actual plottage value increments affecting individual parcels at other assemblages for similar redevelopment ventures. Analysis of an assemblage costing $2,000,000 for 10 similar properties, or $200,000 per parcel, might be 50% greater than the known, recent sales prices of several of the properties. Therefore, it may be reasonable in such instances to add the incremental value to the market value of the individual subject parcels.

The Development Approach as a Value Indicator

The development approach has evolved in recent years into what may be considered a fourth valuation approach. It can be described as the income approach for development projects because it accounts for all cash flows, including revenue and reasonable expenses pertaining to the subject development. Net project revenues are then discounted or capitalized into value indications.

The development approach, like other valuation approaches, can be used improperly, whether the objective of analysis is to test financial feasibility, indicate market or investment value, or project probable cash flow during the ownership or marketing period.

Some typical applications of the development approach are: 1) proposed or existing residential, commercial, recreational, or industrial subdivisions where sites are to be marketed, and 2) condominium projects. Planned unit developments (PUDs) and other multi-use developments are typically analyzed using the development approach, which may be the primary or only reliable value indicator.

The development approach begins with the estimation of anticipated revenue from all sources by month, quarter, or year for the duration of the marketing or holding period. The anticipated costs of ownership and disposition during this period and a reasonable entrepreneurial profit are deducted from the period revenue, and the balance is allocated to existing physical assets or to the estimated costs of construction in instances where improvements are incomplete or nonexistent. The net revenues then are discounted to reflect the time value of money, and this conversion process yields a value indication for the subject property rights.

The development approach is customarily used to derive an indication of market value or investment value, but it uses retail value estimates in the process. It is therefore necessary to clarify the conceptual differences among these terms to eliminate confusion. *Retail value* is the value of a single lot or unit, and the sum of the retail values is appropriately termed *gross retail value* or *gross revenue*; it should never be termed *market value*. The retail value of a single lot or unit, however, will be the market value of that lot or unit because the retail value reflects transactions of similar lots which sold to individual purchasers or users.

The market value of the entire subject property will reflect the same component parts as the individual tracts, but the markets are significantly different. The typical investor in the entire property is influenced by the prospects for profit on each of the components, while the lot purchaser is motivated by benefits of use and occupancy or profits from building.

The following discussion presumes a partially developed PUD in which residential lots are to be marketed to builders or individuals who will construct residences for single-family occupancy and use.

ESTIMATION OF RETAIL VALUE

Because the ultimate resolution of either market value or investment value depends to some degree on the amount of gross revenue, it is important that the retail value of the individual lots be reasonably estimated. The analyst must determine whether the typical purchaser is an individual acquiring one lot or a builder negotiating for a block of lots. If several lots are typically acquired by each purchaser, it may well be that the market provides builder discounts for bulk acquisitions. Additional market research should reveal the effects of any bulk purchase discounts and enable the analyst to reasonably project gross revenue.

If marketing is expected to require several months or years, the analyst must also decide whether revenue will be projected on the basis of current dollars or if the effects of inflation are to be included in the revenue estimate. The distinctions between current and constant dollars were discussed earlier in this section.

ESTIMATION OF MARKETING PERIOD

The validity of the estimated value of the entire inventory depends to a great extent on accurately projecting the probable marketing or sellout period. The projection period is based on analysis and reasonable assumptions regarding the present and anticipated supply of competitive lots or units and price levels at competitive locations.

These factors influence the capture rate, i.e., the rate of anticipated absorption of the subject lots by the market. The market survey may reveal that a certain number of lots or units have been absorbed on average each month for the past month, quarter, year, or years. These facts may be important for historical data analysis, but they may not relate to present and future markets. Population trends may be reversing and household sizes may be changing; various factors may invalidate the use of certain historical indicators, but they must be understood thoroughly to assure reasonably accurate projections.

The absorption rate should also relate to the retail values estimated for the lots or units. If retail value estimates or asking prices are excessive, the marketing period will usually be extended. In ultracompetitive markets where there is an obvious oversupply, the investment may succeed only if retail prices are reduced sufficiently to shorten the projected marketing period. In such instances it is quite possible to reduce retail prices and not substantially reduce the market values of the development package.

ESTIMATION OF OWNERSHIP AND DISPOSITION COSTS

The prudent owner of the development package will be aware of potential costs, including ad valorem taxes on unsold inventory; sale commissions and other marketing expenses; and charges for engineering surveys, legal services, and insurance premiums. In many instances, the project owner will have to expend extraordinary funds for brochure preparation, sale parties, nonrecurring advertising, and various initial marketing efforts.

If the developer/owner elects to employ marketing personnel or to handle the marketing without using licensed agents, there should be a marketing cost allowance in lieu of agents' commissions. If the owner/developer handles all of the marketing personally and no direct out-of-pocket marketing expense is incurred, the appraiser will properly elect to deduct a reasonable estimate for the cost of such marketing services or provide for this expense by increasing the entrepreneurial profit earned by the owner/developer.

DEVELOPMENT COSTS AND ENTREPRENEURIAL PROFIT

The anticipated cost of developing a proposed project or the estimated costs of completing a partially developed one must be deducted from the projected revenue estimate. If the project is developed in several phases and marketing will continue for several years, a prudent owner/developer will expend development funds as necessary to assure a sufficient inventory of lots or units. It may be necessary to incur major expenditures for water, sewage treatment, and recreational facilities early in the development process to maximize the marketing strategies, but installation of streets and utility lines in areas that won't be marketed for several months or years is usually unwarranted.

Deductions for anticipated future installations should be properly reflected in the period of expenditure because investment timing affects the present value of the total project. As previously mentioned, it is important to consistently use present purchasing power or inflated future dollars in estimating costs and revenue.

Entrepreneurial profit is the reward anticipated by the developer/investor for accepting the numerous risks attributable to the venture. The various risks usually relate to uncertainties in estimating or projecting development, holding, and marketing costs; project development and absorption time estimates; and the risks of accurately estimating lot prices months or years hence.

Entrepreneurial rewards usually appear to be directly related to the degree of uncertainty and may be generally estimated at about 15%-25% of the retail sales at such planned developments. There are fewer risks for the investor/developer when all the development costs have been expended and the improvements are installed. Accordingly, the prudent investor/developer of a partially developed project is justified in accepting a lower rate of entrepreneurial profit as there are less significant risks for the improvements previously installed.

DISCOUNTING TO PRESENT WORTH

The various costs for construction, development, marketing, interim financing, and other expenses or allowances are deducted from the total estimate of retail value to derive an indication of the net projected proceeds of the development. It is more desirable and more precise to chart revenue and expenses according to the anticipated period (in months) in which sales are expected to occur.

The net proceeds are discounted to present worth using present worth factors at the appropriately selected discount rate, which must be market-supported if the indicated value is to be labeled market value. The use of an unsupported discount rate or a rate suggested by a client or other interested party would not be market-oriented and would represent an estimate of investment value or value to a specific investor.

If the preceding process is used properly, the market discount rate will typically range from 12%-25% per year, depending on the type of property, the accompanying risks, and whether the allowance for entrepreneurial profit is sufficient. The discount rate should be applied in a manner consistent with the anticipated flow of proceeds. If revenue and expenditures are anticipated on a monthly basis throughout the development and marketing period, monthly discounting would produce the most accurate valuation. This might be impractical if a five- or ten-year period is anticipated; essentially the same conclusions would be derived using quarterly or annual discounting, provided that mid-period factors are selected.

Mid-period factors are usually justified in that most revenues and expenditures occur randomly throughout the periods and the "average" period is an approximation. There is equal probability that revenue and expenditures will occur in the first and second halves of the period.

It may be argued that, in following the preceding format, the appraiser is doubly discounting the proceeds from the sale of lots or units for entrepreneurial profit and for the time value of money. Entrepreneurial profit is an incentive considered necessary to attract a prudent investor/developer and, like any other development cost, it should be deducted from gross revenue. If reasonable entrepreneurial profit is not deducted, the net proceeds will capitalize into an exorbitant and erroneous land value indication, unless the discount rate is adjusted to reflect entrepreneurial risks.

For these reasons, it is of utmost importance to relate the final indication of market value to any available sales of similarly developed tracts. This comparative analysis should reveal discount rates and units of price comparison which could alleviate the embarrassment of omitting one or more of the factors influencing the valuation of complex developments.

The final value conclusion is the estimated value of the property "as is" on the appraisal date. Regardless of the type of present ownership, the value estimate is the dollar amount the typical investor/developer would be justified in paying for the property on that date. The acquisition price will presumably include an agent's commission and the purchaser will anticipate completion of the development and marketing of the units to earn a profit commensurate with the risks inherent in all aspects of the project.

The development approach can be an excellent tool for testing the highest and best use of a parcel of land which is believed to be ready for development. If the discounted land value is not substantially greater than the land value supported by land sales, the land probably should not be developed to the envisioned usage.

Flood-Hazard Land

Appraisers frequently have diverse opinions concerning the market value of flooded, flood-prone, or flood-hazard land. Therefore, it is important to be aware of various factors that should be considered in the analysis and valuation of these lands. Through casual observation, appraisers may conclude that such land areas can or cannot be utilized. Frequently, the appraiser has little or no supportive market data pertaining to these lands. Therefore, it is very important that the potential use, if any, be determined for the flood-hazard land.

Some appraisers have overappraised flood lands while others have underappraised them. With the current emphasis on our environment by public agencies and private groups, the appraiser must be particularly alert to the necessity of thoroughly analyzing the market for such lands.

Canals, floodways, and certain agricultural wetlands may clearly have value in use or economic value, while other flooded, flood-prone, or flood-hazard land may have values ranging from insignificant to substantial. The market value of flood-hazard land, and of more desirable types of land, is primarily dependent upon proper analysis of the land's highest and best use, with consideration for various physical, economic, and governmental factors.

Flood lands include areas that are: 1) permanently flooded by design for public or private purposes, 2) prone to flood frequently, and 3) judged to have a high probability for flooding by natural causes.

Private ponds and public lakes are examples of lands that are intentionally flooded in anticipation of either private or public benefits. These benefits may include recreation, preservation of natural habitats, or production of energy at public floodways. Private floodings are usually designed to provide private or commercial recreational benefits or value appreciation of surrounding land for development and/or marketing.

The floodways controlled by governmental or quasi-governmental agencies are considered to be permanently flooded and maintained for the public's benefit. Certain private floodings, such as those preceding subdivision development and the sale of adjoining lots and recreational use rights, are essentially considered permanently flooded because the developer grants certain floodway rights with the sale of each lot. The pond or lake created for totally private purposes can usually be drained, provided such draining does not adversely affect the rights of others. It is quite possible that the flood site could be restored to its original topographical condition, i.e., its condition prior to the intentional flooding.

Areas that are prone to frequent flooding are usually restricted as to use. Such lands within major municipalities are usually controlled by zoning ordinances which preclude construction of permanent improvements. Flood-prone tracts in rural areas are typically left in their natural states for recreational purposes. Although some of these tracts may not be restricted by zoning ordinances, it is usually not financially feasible to salvage the flood-prone land with extensive landfill efforts. There may be an abundance of vacant land in the area available at low prices.

Urban flood zones frequently are located where land salvage efforts may be financially feasible. However, zoning and planning departments of most communities are under pressure from governmental agencies, private conservation groups, and certain individuals to protect the environment by precluding the development of these lands.

Primary flood areas are those designated by the U.S. Army Corps of Engineers or some related agency as having the statistical probability of flooding at least once during a 50-year period. An intermediate flood plain is an area that has the statistical probability of flooding at least once during a 100-year period. It should be noted that flood zones may change and can be redefined as various upstream, downstream, and local conditions change. These conditions may include the effects of changes in the water table and upstream construction (particularly paved areas), which increase water run-off and reduce ground absorption.

Although most lands located within 50- and 100-year floodplain areas cannot be developed with permanent improvements, most can be used to a limited degree. There is substantial debate and concern that development preclusions are essentially the taking of valuable private property rights without the payment of just compensation. Also, the owner of record is responsible for the annual payment of ad valorem taxes.

Most municipal zoning departments allow the owner of flood land to utilize all or part of the area for nonpermanent construction or for calculation of development densities. This is particularly significant when the parent tract or adjoining land is zoned to permit development of apartments or residential condominiums. Many jurisdictions allow 100% of the flood area to be used for density calculations for development on the parent tract, while others allow 25%–50%.

This allowance essentially enables the non-floodplain part of the parent tract to be developed with more permanent physical improvements than would have been allowed on the parent tract without the floodplain area. In many jurisdictions, the floodplain areas may be used for landscaping, recreation, and automobile parking, provided that flowage areas are not impeded.

The degree of potential use and the market value of flood-prone or flood-hazard land depend on: 1) the present zoning and the probability of rezoning; 2) the size of the parent tract, which includes the floodplain; and 3) the location, configuration, and size of the flood area. Because the floodplain classification can encumber all of the tract or a sufficient area to render the tract useless, the prospects for assemblage with adjoining land becomes an important value consideration.

The market value of floodplain land is probably greater when the land and the parent tract are zoned or can be zoned to permit multifamily residential development. This may be partially due to: 1) the generally low development densities at modern apartment and condominium projects, 2) the relatively small surface area required for building locations as two- or three-level construction is not unusual, and 3) the parking and recreation areas that can usually be placed on floodplain land, provided that residents do not have to walk unreasonable distances between the dwelling units and parking spaces.

Floodplain areas at tracts which will likely be developed for single-family residential, commercial, or industrial purposes generally present more difficult valuation problems. The location and configuration of the floodplain greatly affects its adaptability to development of these property types. If the floodplain areas can be used to create larger, more functional, or more buildable residential sites, then the floodplain acreage may be as valuable as the balance of the tract. With industrial land, subdivision into larger sites with extra truck parking or yard storage may be feasible, depending on the floodplain's location and proximity to the principal building.

Valuation of floodplain land is generally difficult because of the diverse factors previously discussed, as well as the dearth of sales of flood land and the difficulties in allocating sales prices to usable and nonusable (or limited-use) floodplain land for those properties with some flood land.

Sales of exclusive flood land occur infrequently. These lands may be transferred as donations to agencies for park and recreational use, but these transactions seldom provide reliable value indicators. The donor's motivation probably is to obtain a gift deduction and to eliminate the responsibility for paying annual ad valorem taxes. Most sales of floodplain land will be ultraspeculative, unless: 1) the land is acquired by an adjoining owner who anticipates obtaining the benefits of transferring development densities ascribed to the floodplain acreage, 2) the land adjoins a stream or lake and has the potential for use as a hunting or fishing club, or 3) the flood land has potential for growing merchantable timber.

The proper price allocation will likely be affected by the various factors previously discussed as the price should reflect the land's potential for development or use in the eyes of the investor.

Valuation of Partial and Fractional Ownership Interests

In the United States, the conventional "fee simple," which is the most complete and absolute title available, is owned subject to the rights of taxation, eminent domain, police power, and escheat, which are reserved by government. Most types of real property are customarily divided into various physical, legal, and financial interests. These fractional or undivided partial interests are frequently the subject of appraisal assignments, particularly in regard to estate settlement matters or situations where an investor desires or is required to acquire or dispose of ownership.

Ownership interests may be divided physically into land and improvements, legally into various easement and lease interests, and financially into debt and equity. The physical real estate can be further divided horizontally or vertically into legal and financial interests, such as various easements; air rights; and surface, subsurface, and mineral rights. Life estates and purchase/lease options are real property interests, and limited partnership shares are real property/security interests which often require value analysis.

Fractional ownership interests may be voluntarily created by joint acquisition of a property right as tenants in common, or by acquisition of stock in a corporation or entity holding title or shares of a limited partnership. Fractional interests can be created involuntarily by the death of an owner and subsequent inheritance by his/her heirs.

"Fractional," "undivided" and "partial" interests are customarily used synonymously, but the terms may differ in degree. For purposes of this discussion, *partial* ownership is construed to signify ownership representing less than 100% of the fee simple interest. Various leaseholds, easements, mortgages, equity interests, horizontal and vertical rights, and rights pertaining to timber or minerals are also considered partial interests.

Fractional or *undivided* interests are all partial because they relate to either partial rights or multiple ownership of a particular interest or right. For example, a leasehold interest in a warehouse or the title to a dwelling unit in a multi-story condominium is a partial interest, but it will also be a fractional or undivided interest if it is owned by more than one entity.

This chapter will explore various factors that may influence the value of partial or fractional ownership interests. There are many circumstances, particularly in estate settlement or trust/portfolio management, where reasonable estimation of the value for taxation or marketing purposes is mandatory and/or practicable.

The market value of a property interest may be less or greater than the mathematical proration of the interest relative to the entire ownership. The market value estimate is a function of perceived "marketability," which is directly influenced by the type and degree of ownership interest involved.

Although most of this discussion relates to conventional real property rights owned by various entities, including simple and limited partnerships, joint tenancy, and tenancy in common, limited partnerships are considered securities and are specifically addressed later in this chapter.

The market value of the entire fee simple ownership should not be affected by the form of ownership, but ownership can have a substantial impact on the marketability, and consequently the market value, of an undivided or partial ownership interest. Therefore, primary consideration must be afforded the factors affecting marketability.

The prudent general investor in an undivided interest recognizes that major investment decisions regarding management, operations, leasing, financing, and development or redevelopment will involve other individuals who may not be similarly motivated. Accordingly, there may be great potential for disagreement or disharmony among the partners, which could have a detrimental effect on the profitability or use of the subject real estate.

Investors frequently own real property jointly, but individual shares or interests seldom transfer except to existing partners. More frequently, the entire ownership transfers to unrelated parties, but such transactions usually do not reflect market value indications for those individual or separate interests.

Because of various uncertainties as to ownership, management, and other factors, prospective puchasers generally are quite reluctant to acquire an undivided interest. The magnitude of their concern directly affects the amount of price discount or premium that will be acceptable to the buyer or seller.

A prudent prospective investor will attempt to define the risks inherent in the property and the form of ownership. An ownership interest involving a duplex residence will usually generate more investor concern than a share in the ownership of a regional shopping center. The smaller investment property will probably involve very few people, and no seasoned investors, while the larger investment may involve more partners with substantial financial capabilities and skills.

The specific individuals represented in the partnership or ownership entity may have a significant impact on its marketability. The prudent investor may be motivated to pay a premium for a fractional interest if one or more of the present owners is famous; one might not be interested at any price if one of the owners is known to be without integrity. Of course, the property interest might be quite marketable at par to another person of low integrity.

The size of the available interest may also be a significant factor. A minute share may be highly marketable, or have a premium market value because of the power the small ownership has in making investment decisions. As with the assemblage of land parcels, the complete assemblage of ownership interests may be thwarted by a minor shareholder. On the other hand, the ownership share may be so large that marketability is impaired. In this case, consideration should be given to the prospect of dividing the share into smaller, more marketable investment units.

The author recognizes at least three detrimental factors frequently inherent in the ownership of a fractional real property interest:

1. The longer period required to market a fractional interest, as contrasted with a total ownership interest;
2. Difficulties in obtaining a consensus among partners in the management of affairs; and
3. Difficulties in the underwriting of loans on real property involving fractional interests. Most lenders will require the guaranty or personal endorsement of each partner, and some partners may be reluctant to accept the obligation for the ownership entity.

Fractional ownership interests may sell at par or even at premiums in transactions where the ultimate owners are friends or business associates or in certain instances where one partner is a figure of notoriety. However, the appraiser of market value must assume a sale in the open market to a typical purchaser, not a particular individual or entity.

The market value of a fractional interest in real property is the pro rata share of the total market value of the property plus a value adjustment for any detrimental or beneficial factors inherent in the fractional ownership.

In appraising fractional interests, as in valuing full ownership, sales and other market data are desirable value indicators. If these market data are available, they should be analyzed with consideration for the various factors previously presented.

In the absence of reliable and usable market data, the appraiser must judge whether the ownership interest is likely to sell for a price premium. One method for estimating an ascribable value discount is to consider the effects of the longer marketing period as compared with the typical period necessary for marketing the entire ownership. The pro rata value multiplied by the factor representing the present worth of the right to receive $1.00 at the end of the excess or additional marketing period—at the market-derived discount rate—is the indicated market value of the fractional interest.

For example, assume the market value of a full ownership is $663,000; the proration for a one-quarter undivided interest is $165,750. The subject ownership interest is projected to require 18 months for marketing, or approximately 12 months more than the six months judged necessary to market the entire real property. Current research confirms that this "excess" marketing period is reasonable and market supportable. A discount rate of 12% per annum is considered reasonable. The factor representing the present worth of the right to receive $1.00 at the end of one year, with discounting at 12% per annum, is 0.8929.

The indicated value of the fractional interest is calculated:

$$\$165{,}750 \times 0.8929 = \$148{,}000$$

This reflects a value discount of approximately 10% for the negative characteristics of the one-quarter fractional ownership.

LIMITED PARTNERSHIPS

Limited partnership shares relating to real property are generally considered securities, but their proper valuation will require analysis of the pertinent real property.

Most limited partnerships are governed by a partnership agreement, which gives the general partner sole management responsibility. Decisions pertaining to disposition, development, financing, additional partners, and other matters may require a shareholder vote representing a majority of ownership interest.

Limited partnerships are typically formed by a general partner, who invites various prospective investors to participate in a specific venture. Frequently, the partners do not know each other well, but rely on the general partner's experience and reputation as a promoter, manager, or developer. Perhaps the most significant characteristic of a limited partnership is that management is relegated to the general partner. Because most partners were not very close when the group was formed, the addition or substitution of a partner will probably not be very noticeable or controversial, unless the prospective investor is known to be of questionable repute.

The orginal partners were selected by the general partner, so the new or replacement partners will probably be selected in the same way. Therefore, it is questionable whether the sale of a partnership interest satisfies the assumptions inherent in the market value definition. Caution must be exercised when analyzing sales of partnership interests. These sales reflect reasonable price expectations, but the final estimate can hardly be called market value unless it satisfies the definition's requisites.

Valuation of partnership assets in fee simple is a natural beginning point for the valuation of an ownership share. The pro rata share allocation provides a benchmark before adjustment for any market reluctance is made.

The partnership agreement typically stipulates conditions for settling disputes, management powers, and payment for contracted services. If a partner dies, substitution of the estate's agent or representative is usually provided. The properly drafted agreement also provides for the treatment of partnership shares in the event a partner elects either to discontinue funding or to sell his shares. The partnership may have the right of first refusal to buy the shares at a price less than the pro rata share value or at a predetermined percentage of the capital invested. The general partner may have the vested authority to make the final determination regarding the ultimate ownership of the share.

It is quite likely that the partnership share will have less marketability to potential outside investors if the partnership or its individual partners elect not to buy it. Reduced marketability will strongly suggest a basis for substantially reducing the market value of a partnership unit/share.

Diligent research is necessary to establish reasonable price relationships between the subject property and other limited partnership properties with similar characteristics. In the absence of such data, the factors presented here and other factors likely to affect the marketability of the specific ownership share should be reflected in the final value estimate.

EASEMENT VALUE CONSIDERATIONS

Easements are generally defined as the right of one party (the dominant or beneficial estate) to use a prescribed surface, subsurface, or airspace of another party (the subservient estate). Easements may be acquired for the exclusive use of the dominant or beneficial estate, or they may be nonexclusive and jointly used by the beneficial and subservient estates. Easements are a form of partial ownership in real estate acquired by contract negotiation, by prescriptive use, or through authorized eminent domain proceedings.

The numerous types and kinds of easements can be generally classified as either temporary or permanent in nature. This factor is a major determinant in establishing the value of a specific easement to the beneficial estate or the effect of the easement on the subservient estate. Because easements transfer provisional use or control, they represent partial ownership interests. Many easements detrimentally affect the residual value of the subservient estate, which includes the encumbered area and the benefitting area located outside the defined easement. Accordingly, the market value of the fee simple interest may not equal the sum of the values of the beneficial and subservient estates.

The real property appraiser may be confronted with the task of estimating: 1) the market value of the subservient estate or property as presently encumbered, 2) the value of a proposed beneficial easement, or 3) the effects of a proposed easement on the encumbered estate. A dominant easement may be extremely valuable when the property's continued or prospective use depends on the easement for access. The easement may have special value to the beneficial estate which exceeds the fee simple value of the underlying land at the encumbered location.

Valuation of beneficial interests in a particular easement or the effects of such an easement on the subservient estate would ideally be supported by recent sales of similar easement rights or properties similarly encumbered, from which easement values might be imputed. However, most easements are acquired by negotiation under threat of condemnation through eminent domain, so the respective settlement prices are not usually considered reasonable "arm's length" value indicators. Although sales of similar subservient estates may be analyzed to suggest the effects of a similar easement on the encumbered remainder parcel, such analysis would reflect any consequential or severance damages. Accordingly, the price analysis might have little or no bearing on the value of the easement.

The appraiser should determine if the proposed or prospective easement is for private, public, or quasi-public use. The private beneficial estate will be acquired through negotiations and this acquisition cost/price may be a value indicator for other similar easement appraisals. Acquisition attempts for public and quasi-public easements usually begin with negotiation efforts, but all parties are aware that the agency can and will resort to authorized eminent domain proceedings if negotiations are not successful. In the absence of reliable market data for easement value indicators, the appraiser must use simple logic. This frequently creates additional dilemmas because the appraiser's reasoning may not be admissable as evidence in courts of law. Some of the major factors which should influence the appraiser's value conclusions are:

1. The temporary or perpetual nature of the easement.
2. The probability of continual interruption and use for maintenance or additional construction within the easement area, and any possible pollution from noise, dust, etc.
3. The hazards of the easement improvements (or use) to the neighborhood and/or the subservient parcel.
4. The subservient owner's capacity to continue using the encumbered area, subject to the rights of the beneficial estate.
5. The size, shape, and location of the easement.
6. The size, shape, and utility of the "remainder" subservient estate.
7. Any noted limitations on redevelopment, such as changing economic use or increased costs of construction in, over, beneath, or near the easement area.
8. Any other detrimental effects of the easement and related use/improvements on the subservient estate.
9. The financial responsibility for payment of ad valorem taxes and other expenses attributable to the encumbered area.

Permanent easement values are typically expressed as a percentage of the fee simple value, after consideration has been given to the preceding factors. The easement value may range from about 5% to 100%; a 100% value indicates essentially a fee taking. It is considered quite possible for the easement "taking" to exceed the fee simple value in instances where the subservient estate continues to be responsible for all ad valorem taxes on the encumbered property. This can only occur, however, when the nature of the easement excludes the subservient estate from use of the encumbered area. Examples of such an occurrence might include permanent flowage or flood easements, restricted access easements for ingress and egress, or major utility easements for substations or traversing trunk lines on parcels in urban, high-density locations.

Utility easements vary in magnitude, complexity, and impact, whether beneficial or detrimental, on the subservient estates. Utility easements are usually permanent in nature and may be service-oriented or used as a trunk line to transport the utility to another area. Subsurface and aerial service utility lines in urban areas are customarily located in easements along streets or roads and typically provide some benefit to the subservient estate. These easements are usually nonexclusive as the subservient estate owner continues to use the encumbered area for landscaping or driveway purposes. In most instances, the easement areas parallel the street and are included within the required building setback, which precludes more intense development. Accordingly, the easement value typically represents a small portion of the fee simple value.

Trunk utility and pipeline easements traversing rural areas do not usually benefit the subservient estate. Aerial and subsurface easements and related installations do not usually preclude cattle grazing or the growing of various crops in rural areas or the use of paved parking in urban areas, provided that the beneficial easement is not affected. The beneficial estate holder can usually enter the easement area at will for maintenance, to modify the magnitude and type of improvements in accordance with the easement agreement, and to police for violations that may affect the improvements installed within the easement.

Utility poles in the easement may create difficulties in maneuvering farm equipment and certain dangers may exist near high-voltage electric transmission lines or certain pipeline installations. Pipelines are heavy construction, but line breaks can occur and cause disaster or disruption of subservient estate activities. High-voltage electric transmission lines are constructed on huge, unsightly aerial towers and frequently affect land use plans for development of tracts near towns and business centers. The transmission of energy on these lines may cause television reception interference and may attract lightning, a hazard to people and livestock.

Extensive research may be required and market data pertaining to similar tracts with and without encumbering easements should be obtained for analysis. The effects of major traversing easements on tract development may require additional analysis by land planners and market studies by the appraiser.

There is another form of aerial easement for public streets and expressway viaducts which occupy air rights in urban centers. This construction typically does not preclude development or use of surface, subsurface, or higher elevation air rights, provided that the aerial easement is not affected. The aerial easement will usually include the right to construct necessary support structures through lower air space to the ground surface. The effects of such an easement are properly evaluated through analysis of sales, leases, and net income projections for the site development before and after the easement.

Avigation easements pertain to the rights of aircraft to traverse prescribed airspace through descending and ascending elevations near airport facilities. Avigation easements restrict construction or installation of buildings, radio/T.V. towers, or antennae above established elevations within the easement. In the absence of market transactions, net income projections for the site developed with buildings with and without height restrictions should be discounted to properly measure value differences which will indicate the easement value and any damages.

Access easements for ingress or egress are typically private in nature and may be negotiated for joint use by the beneficial and subservient estates, or for exclusive use by the beneficial estate. Access rights are particularly useful and valuable to a parcel that is landlocked or has remote or circuitous primary accessibility. The value of an access easement to the beneficial estate can be measured as the incremental value created by the improved access. The value of the easement should be less than fee simple value, presuming the subservient estate retains joint use and ownership. It is quite likely that the beneficial estate owner will be pressured during private negotiations to pay a premium price for the easement, particularly when substantial benefits are apparent and the premium is justified.

Certain temporary easement values are more readily estimated using "fair return" analysis. This procedure is particularly applicable in the valuation of temporary construction, drainage, or slope easements of a specified duration. The suggested process necessitates the estimation of unit land value in fee simple, the effective rate of periodic return, and the encumbrance period.

In most markets, land value estimates for the total tract in fee simple can be reasonably supported and the period of easement can be ascertained within limits. The fair rate of return may be most difficult to derive and support; it usually requires consideration of discount rates reflected by sales of dissimilar, but competitive, properties and analysis of yields on bonds, stocks, and mortgages. The selected fair rate of return is even more controversial because: 1) the nature of the temporary easement is short-term, 2) the fee owner will presumably continue to be responsible for the payment of ad valorem taxes, 3) the "rent" will probably be treated as ordinary income for federal tax reporting purposes, and 4) the rate should provide for any additional management made necessary by the easement. Sales and lease analyses of improved or unimproved tracts will reflect *net* rates of return on investments and capital gain prospects. Also, the rate analyses reflect investment characteristics for fee simple market value and do not reflect possible consequential or severance damages which might accompany the easement. Accordingly, in selecting the ultimate rate of return, the appraiser should be aware of these investment vagaries and dissimilarities.

For example, consider a construction easement that is scheduled to encumber one acre of a larger tract for a three-year period. The easement area will be used to store tools, equipment, and supplies during construction of a public project, and no damages are likely to be suffered by the subservient site during construction or after completion of the project. The fee simple land value is estimated at $10,000 per acre, and the land to be encumbered is representative of the parent tract. Although improved sales analysis typically reflects a 10% net rate of return on investment, the rate of return is estimated at 12% per year "gross," because the subservient estate is responsible for ad valorem taxes and some degree of management. The temporary easement value is calculated:

Fee value of easement area (1 acre)	$10,000
Fair annual rate of return	× .12
Annual return	$ 1,200
Present worth factor for the anticipated 3-year easement period (payment in advance)	× 2.6900
Estimated easement value	$3,228
Rounded	$3,250

This discussion of easements and valuation is not sufficiently comprehensive to address all of the numerous types of easements which exist. However, it can be concluded that most permanent easements can be valued either by comparative market data analysis or by income capitalization to reflect value differences with and without easements. Temporary easements can seldom be reliably appraised by analyses of market transactions; the estimation of a fair return on fee simple value for the easement duration is considered to be more plausible and defensible. Nevertheless, available market data may lend strength to easement value analysis and conclusions derived by other methods and techniques.

The appraiser should be careful, particularly in appraising permanent easements, to avoid estimating easement values as a percentage of fee simple value without the support of market data or logic. The final easement value should consider the relative magnitude of property rights acquired by use, impact (damages), or continual financial support by the subservient estate. Redistribution of all major property rights from the fee estate to the beneficial easement holder essentially transfers fee simple ownership, and the final easement value should be judged accordingly. ◻